MISSION FURNITURE
YOU CAN BUILD

MISSION FURNITURE
YOU CAN BUILD

By John D. Wagner

HOUGHTON MIFFLIN COMPANY
BOSTON   NEW YORK   1997

For information about permission to reproduce selections from this book, write to Permissions, Houghton Mifflin Company, 215 Park Avenue South, New York, New York 10003.

Library of Congress Cataloging-in-Publication Data

Wagner, John D., 1957-
    Mission furniture you can build : authentic techniques and designs for the home woodworker / by John D. Wagner ; photography by Andrew Kline ; illustrations by Barbara Smullen.
        p.   cm.
    ISBN 1-57630-040-4 (paperback)
    1. Furniture making—Amateurs' manuals. 2. Furniture, Mission.
    I. Title.
    TT195.W34 1997   97-15962
    684.1'04—dc21   CIP

Printed in the United States of America

DOC 10 9 8 7 6 5 4 3 2 1

Designed by Eugenie S. Delaney
Front and back covers and inside photographs (except on page 17) by Andrew Kline

This book is dedicated to the memory of my mother,

Patricia Coyle Wagner (1930–1996),

and to my wife, Leita Millay Hancock.

ACKNOWLEDGMENTS

I couldn't have written this book without the love and support of my dear family, including my wife, Leita; my dear dad, John F. Wagner; and all my brothers, sisters and relations: Carole, Dennis, Paul, Mark, Monica, Chris, Judy, Mary Pat, Greg, Barbara and The B; Julia, Gregory, Alyse, Martha, Olivia, Tynan, Natasha, Shiobhan, Dan, Mac, Loni, Tom, Joe, Joan, Mara and Tracy. I especially want to thank my loving uncles Gene and Richard for all they've done for me. A heartfelt thanks to you all.

I have also been blessed with many friends who have been indefatigable in their support for me during the writing of this book and in the years previous to it, including John and Gail Puleio, David Dobbs, Duf Gallagher, Clayton and Sally DeKorne, and Marylee MacDonald — *simpatico*.

I also want to thank the following people for their help in producing this book: my editor, Sandy Taylor, who brought me to this project; Emily Stetson, the copy editor; Eugenie Delaney, the book designer; Barbara Smullen, the illustrator; Brooks Banker, whose interest in Mission furniture inspired mine; and Barry Estabrook and James Lawrence, for backing the project.

And I especially thank the woodworkers who produced most of the furniture photographed in this book: Grant Taylor (Lamson Taylor Doors, Tucker Rd., South Acworth, NH); Sam Kinghorn (All Things Considered, 11 Maple St., Essex Junction, VT); and Ron Miller (P.O. Box 363, Dublin, NH).

C O N T E N T S

INTRODUCTION

Gustav Stickley
and the Arts and Crafts Movement

The Mission furniture plans in this book are simplified versions of plans originally presented to the public by Gustav Stickley (1858-1942), the master designer and builder of Mission furniture. As part of his efforts to publicize his Craftsman furniture and put forth an aesthetic of "noble work," Stickley published a magazine called *The Craftsman*, from 1901 to 1916 (see Fig. 1). That's where the original plans first appeared.

Stickley initially published the plans for schoolchildren, because he believed that they needed to be trained to work with their hands as well as their heads. He called his approach "manual training," and to encourage that training, he offered scale drawings of furniture pieces that were meant to be copied (see Fig. 2). By presenting sim-

Fig. 1 The Craftsman *magazine's first issue featured an homage to William Morris, a major influence on Gustav Stickley. A leading voice of the Arts and Crafts movement, the magazine remained in print from October 1901 to December 1916.*

ilar plans in this book in an attempt to develop the reader's carpentry skills, we enter into a grand tradition of furniture building that would have greatly pleased Stickley, for this is what he envisioned.

If you compare the drawings Stickley presented in *The Craftsman* magazine to the furniture that Stickley was producing at that time in his Eastwood, New York, shops, you'll find the plans and the furniture are strikingly similar. Though it seems odd, Stickley was essentially giving away his trade secrets and encouraging people to build the very furniture he was trying to sell. In modern times, where company secrets are the subject of international espionage, and patents are guarded with expensive court battles, this seems unfathomable. But the fact that Stickley would give away his designs was a testament to how strongly he believed in this principle of "manual training," that the citizenry, *especially* its youngsters, should be educated in heart and head to employ noble work, using natural materials, and—as a result of this training—be better equipped morally and spiritually to live honest, democratic lives. Stickley's approach was essentially holistic, even religious.

Using his magazine, *The Craftsman*, Stickley branched out into areas other than furniture, and went on to publish articles on gardening, landscaping, poetry and cultural issues—even Native American arts. The articles were accompanied by Arts and Crafts philosophy, profiles of master designers and, later, renderings of Craftsman houses, the plans for which Stickley initially gave away, free for the asking.

*T*he Craftsman was one of a number of publications that emerged around the turn of the century to give voice to the new, important movement called Arts and Crafts, only one aspect of which was Stickley's furniture shops. "I did not realize at the time," Stickley wrote, commenting on his involvement in the Arts and Crafts movement, "that in making those few pieces of strong, simple furniture I had started a new movement. Others saw it and prophesied a far-reaching development. To me it was only furniture; to them it was religion. And eventually it became religion with me as well."

The Arts and Crafts movement, of which Stickley was an integral part and eventually one of its leading proponents, ran roughly from 1890 to 1916, with the great flurry of American activity beginning around the turn of the century. As with many movements of this era, whether they were political, literary or aesthetic, American initiatives were in reaction to European and British trends, practices, styles and designs. Even a cursory comparison of European and American events shows how the two cultures were becoming a study in contrasts. Whereas in Europe, Joseph Conrad published *Lord Jim* in 1900, America's Jack London published *The Call of the Wild* just three years later. As Edward VII succeeded Queen Victoria to the throne in 1900, Theodore Roosevelt was elected president. In the worlds of architecture, design and art, shifts of great magnitude were underway, led by dynamic American personalities. By 1889, a young Frank Lloyd Wright (1867-1959) was making a name for himself, and Elbert Hubbard (1856-1915)—the charismatic soap salesman, marketing genius and early proponent of the early Arts and Crafts movement

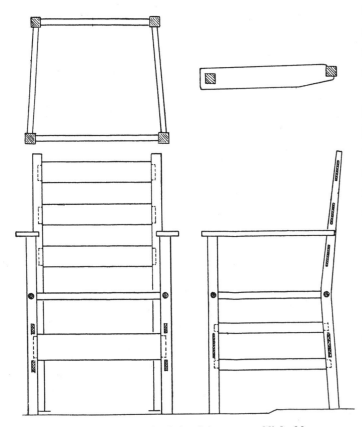

Fig. 2 *These scale chair plans were published by Gustav Stickley in the January 1904 issue of his magazine* **The Craftsman** *in an effort to teach readers, especially young men, how to work with their hands. The poke-through tenons are examples of classic Stickley features.*

(he died on the *Lusitania*)—founded the Roycroft Community craft shops and publishing center three years later. Stickley's first efforts to design and make furniture began in 1897 with his Craftsman Workshops; *The Craftsman* magazine followed in 1901. At this same time, Charles Greene (1868-1957) and Henry Greene (1870-1954), two dynamic architects (who also happened to be brothers), proved capable of heretofore unimaginable architectural innovation with their landmark design of the lyric Gamble House in Pasadena, California.

Though the Arts and Crafts movement blossomed around the turn of the century, it had its origins in a reaction against the industrialization and mechanization of the Industrial Revolution, which marks its beginnings just before James Watt's invention of the steam engine in 1769. In fact, Stickley's design aesthetic, the materials and machines he used and even his relationship to his employee craftsmen and those who purchased his furniture are all part of a lineage whose roots were planted in the fertile soil of a backlash against the Industrial Revolution.

The Industrial Revolution (1750-1850) saw changes of enormous magnitude in economic conditions and structures, as the world witnessed within those hundred years a foundation-shaking transition from small-scale, stable agricultural and local commercial communities, which had their roots in medieval times, to full-blown modern industrialism. The imperial and colonial voyagers of the European powers during the fifteenth and sixteenth centuries had opened the way to worldwide commerce, and these same countries (especially England) intended to grow rich producing and selling its commodities both at home and abroad. But this meant mass production and machines, including Watt's steam engine, Arkwright's spinning frame and Cartwright's power loom. By the time of London's Great Exhibition of 1851, which was intended to celebrate the Industrial Revolution, many leading philosophers and writers of the day,

some of whom would dramatically influence Stickley, expressed distaste for what industrialism had wrought: a worldwide economy dependent on material goods, poisonous by-products, dehumanized workers and shoddy, poorly designed, mass-produced products.

Around 1850, the reaction against the Industrial Revolution found voice in the Gothic Revival movement, which saw as its worthy goal a return to medieval standards of morality and craftsmanship, often centered around the "craftsman guild" collective (all these principles Stickley would adapt in one form or another during his life). The Gothic Revival movement was joined by the Pre-Raphaelite painters, artists of similar instincts who sought to lead simpler lives among well-crafted products that were produced by hand.

Around this time, the English critic John Ruskin (1819-1900) emerged, advocating for the Gothic Revival principles: simple beauty, utility and honest treatment of natural materials. As an art professor at Oxford University, he had considerable influence with his writings as he argued for the value and integrity of the individual, a return to English vernacular designs, the throwing off of anything foreign and the elimination of machine-made goods. As heretical as it may have seemed at that time of dingy, Victorian coal-mining villages and overcrowded cities packed with poor people and blanketed by pollution, Ruskin took the position that work was meant to be full of joy. In 1860 he even denounced greed as the deadly principle guiding English life. Around the same time that Charles Dickens published *Hard Times* (1851), set in the northern industrial city of Coketown, Ruskin published *Seven Lamps of Architecture* (1849) and *The Stones of Venice* (1851). Both books took

> *"The sole consideration at the basis of design must be the thing itself and not its ornamentation."*
>
> GUSTAV STICKLEY

Ruskin's principles of integrating physical and intellectual labors and applied them to design and architecture; both books were to profoundly influence Gustav Stickley.

Also during this period, another major influence on Stickley emerged: William Morris (1834-1896). This English artist, writer, printer and socialist, who studied with the painter Rossetti, was so dramatically influenced by Ruskin's writings that he gave up his plans for the ministry and set out to change society through arts and crafts. Though Morris would become an equally influential thinker, he was—like Stickley—an influential furniture designer as well, whose design aesthetic was a reaction against not only the dehumanizing effects of the Industrial Revolution, but also Victorian design, with its love of anecdotal themes and florid patterns (often carved by machines and then mass-produced).

> *"Have nothing in your houses that you do not know to be useful, or believe to be beautiful."*
>
> WILLIAM MORRIS,
> HOPES AND FEARS
> FOR ART (1882)

In England in 1861, Morris set up his shop using the same medieval craftsman's guild model that Stickley would later emulate in New York. Morris employed medieval craft techniques and natural materials in the making of his products, which included furniture and crafts such as glass works, tiles and fabrics. The Morris chair presented in this book (see page 116), though of Stickley's design, is named after William Morris, and was first produced in his shop in 1866. This is probably the single most popular piece of furniture to come out of the Arts and Crafts movement, but the irony is that Morris did not actually design the chair; he copied it. After Warrington Taylor, Morris's business manager, spotted a chair he liked in a carpenter's shop in Sussex, England, Taylor had Morris's in-house architect, Philip Webb, draw up some plans, which Morris improved upon. William Morris & Co., the name of Morris's firm at the time, started producing the chair, whose popularity immediately caught on. Stickley himself adapted the design, and he first offered it around 1901, claiming that it was "a big chair that means comfort to a tired man when he comes home after the day's work."

As the end of the century neared, Gothic Revival waned in favor of this new aesthetic, Arts and Crafts—the seeds of which Ruskin and Morris planted and nurtured. By 1888, the Arts and Crafts Exhibition Society was organizing events to demonstrate the beauty and popularity of this movement. By then, Arts and Crafts had taken hold, and its proponents urged an integral connection between art and labor, and the designer and the craftsman. In fact, the emerging Arts and Crafts aesthetic was embodied in unified, whole-house environments, where everything from the structure and wall treatments right down to the fixtures and furniture was part of a theme. This notion was central to Stickley's furniture design and especially to his Craftsman house designs of later years. This also became the guiding design principle for the world's most innovative architects: Americans Greene and Greene, Frank Lloyd Wright and designer Harvey Ellis (1852-1904); the Englishmen M. H. Baillie Scott (1865-1945) and C. F. A. Voysey (1857-1941); and the Scottish architect and artist Charles Rennie Mackintosh (1868-1928). The movement that Gustav Stickley would do so much to popularize in America was now in full flower.

The eldest son of a large German immigrant family of humble means, Gustav Stickley (see Fig. 3) came to furniture making by chance, and not, as William Morris had, by virtue of privilege and the deliberate intention to act out an aesthetic developed in the halls of a university. Stickley's father was a stonemason, who got into trouble with drinking and left his family to fend for themselves in the early 1870s. To help support the family, Gustav left school by the eighth grade and went to work for his uncle, Jacob Schlaeger, who owned a small chair factory in Pennsylvania. Stickley later said that it was this job with his uncle that first taught him an appreciation of woodworking and instilled in him a love of the natural grains and patterns of wood.

Stickley's brief stint at his uncle's factory ended when he and his brothers Charles and Albert opened their own furniture wholesale and retail business in Binghamton, New York, in 1884. They sold Shaker furniture and chairs designed and built by their backer, Schuyler C. Brandt.

Just two years later, in 1886, the Stickley Brothers Company started making chairs of its own design. This is the date and event that some historians believe mark the beginning of Craftsman products and the Mission furniture period. To get the undercapitalized business going, Stickley rented time on a broom maker's lathe and turned out some chairs made in the Shaker style. He also produced, as he put it, "some of the simplest and best models of the Old Colonial, Windsor and other plain chairs." It is interesting to think what Stickley would have produced had he not been broke and had access to woodworking machines. His lack of access to machines by necessity forced him to make very simple products, and one would guess from looking at his life's work that he gained an enduring

Fig. 3 *Gustav Stickley (1858-1942) became a leading American advocate for the Arts and Crafts movement and was the designer of the most admired Mission or Craftsman furniture of the time.*

affection for a plain style. As Stickley recalled of that period, "I hired the use of this [lathe] and with it blocked out the plainer parts of some very simple chairs.... All we had was a hand lathe, boring machine, framing saw and chuck, and the power transmitted by rope from a neighboring establishment." Little did Stickley know that he was starting down a road that would lead him to design a furniture line that would become an American classic, collected worldwide, and for which movie stars and wealthy collectors would compete fiercely at high-class auctions just 40 years after his death.

In 1889, Gustav Stickley left his Stickley Brothers Company and teamed up with Elgin A. Simmonds to produce another line of chairs, again in the American Colonial and Shaker modes. But that business soon faded away, and from 1892 to 1894, Stickley was director of manufacturing operations at the New York State Prison in Auburn, New York, where, according to *The New York Times*, he designed that prison's electric chair.

In 1892, Stickley's furniture career sputtered to life again when he and Simmonds formed the Stickley-Simmonds Company, based in Eastwood, New York. It is this site that was later home to the Craftsman Workshops, where Stickley produced his finest and most famous work; but at this point in his career, Stickley was yet to bring forth his line of Mission furniture that he would call "Craftsman." Then in 1899, at 40 years of age, he severed his relationship with Simmonds after six years of partnership.

It was around this time, after Stickley's fits and starts with the business world, that he made a trip to Europe. In his own writings, Stickley makes clear that his Craftsman design came after 1900, after this seminal journey. Given what we know of Stickley, that he had read and admired Morris and Ruskin (he would dedicate the first two issues, respectively, of his magazine, *The Craftsman*, to them), surely he was drawn to Europe to encounter firsthand what influenced them. But the trip must have made their thoughts ring especially true for Stickley, because upon his return, his furniture designs changed dramatically. Perhaps Stickley felt chided when in Europe he looked around at the overflorid, machine-wrought architecture and furniture designed in the year Queen Victoria died, and recalled (or read for the first time) Ruskin's three rules of design, as set forth in his book *The Stones of Venice*:

> *"... to be counted off into a heap of mechanism, numbered with its wheels, and weighed with its hammer strokes—this nature bade not—this humanity for no long time is able to endure."*
>
> JOHN RUSKIN,
> *THE STONES OF VENICE* (1851)

"(1) Never encourage the manufacture of any article not absolutely necessary, in the production of which invention has no share. (2) Never demand an exact finish for its own sake, but only for some practical or noble end. (3) Never encourage imitation or copying of any kind except for the sake of preserving records of great works."

Given that Stickley had spent his life copying other styles and works, these words must have come terribly to life upon visiting England. Morris, Stickley's other influence, echoed Ruskin's theme with his curt proclamation: "Don't copy any style at all, but make your own."

As Stickley was to write retrospectively, "In 1900 I stopped using the standard patterns and finishes, and began to make all kinds of furniture of my own design, independently of what other people were doing, or of any necessity to fit my designs, woods, and finishes to any other factory.... The sole consideration at the basis of design must be the thing itself and not its ornamentation.

"The Arts and Crafts movement was more nearly in harmony with what I had in mind, but even that did not involve a return to the sturdy and primitive forms that were meant for usefulness alone, and I began to work along the lines of a direct application of the fundamental principles of structure to the designing and craftsmanship of my furniture."

Stickley had found religion. In July 1900, following his manifesto to create "sturdy and primitive forms," Stickley exhibited a new line of furniture in Grand Rapids, Michigan. Its Mission design was a radical departure from his earlier work, but it was well received. There is some debate, however, about whether these primitive Mission forms originated with Stickley or if he had seen them elsewhere.

In 1894, six years before Stickley went to Europe, a New York furniture manufacturer named Joseph McHugh had constructed furniture of a primitive form. These designs were based on yet another previous style: The furniture found in the sixteenth-century Franciscan missions of California, which was Spanish in style because of the cultural heritage of the furniture makers, the proselytizing monks from Spain, yet rough in a medieval fashion because the monks did not have access to woodworking machines or fine tools. McHugh exhibited this furniture in his New York Popular Shop, and he called it "Mission." Stickley could well have seen the Mission-style furniture and made note of it, or it could have spontaneously emerged on Stickley's sketch pad and drafting tables at the same time it did on McHugh's by consequence of the spirit of the fin de siècle.

By the end of 1900, Stickley had rented space in the Syracuse, New York, Crouse Stables, where he located a showroom and office to present the furniture his craftsmen were producing in nearby Eastwood. It was here, too, that he first launched his magazine, *The Craftsman*. (Though Mission furniture was the popular name that stuck, Stickley always preferred to call his furniture Craftsman, a name he trademarked.) As Morris in England had done, and as Ruskin had advocated, Stickley set up his furniture workshop modeled after the medieval guild crafts center. And again echoing Morris and Ruskin's hearkening back to a medieval time of simplicity, honest intent and hand crafts, Stickley adopted as his symbol a medieval joiner's compass (see Fig. 4). The motto within the compass is *Als ik kan*, translated from the German as "as I can" or from the original Flemish, "the best I can." This is a motto that Morris himself used, but which he borrowed—like his chair design— this time from the Flemish painter Jan van Eyck. As Stickley himself said, "In the Middle Ages, that golden period of the arts and crafts, each master-workman adopted some device or legend which, displayed upon every object of his creation, came finally to represent his individuality as completely as did his face, or his voice; making him known beyond the burgher [sic] circle in which he passed his life...."

This symbol and slogan appeared in various forms throughout Stickley's life on everything his shops produced. It is this symbol that causes contemporary collectors' hearts to flutter with barely restrainable panic when it is discovered on chair backs at flea markets or in rural antique stores; this symbol that causes checkbooks to open at auctions nationwide, as hard-to-find but increasingly popular authentic Stickley pieces bring higher and higher prices.

Fig. 4 *Stickley's motto "as I can" (in German) is written within a medieval joiner's compass. The slogan and the joiner's compass design hearken back to a time of noble work and honest, simple products.*

By 1901, Stickley had reached his stride, and the years between 1901 and 1905 saw his business flourish. *The Craftsman* was a leading and respected advocate for the Arts and Crafts movement, which had gained substantial currency in America. As his Craftsman pieces gained notoriety, Stickley's furniture was the choice recommended by such architects as Frank Lloyd Wright and the Greene brothers when clients couldn't afford to have furniture designed specifically for themselves.

With increasing popularity came increased competition as Stickley inspired imitators. Among the fiercest were his own brothers. In 1891, Charles and Albert Stickley had started the Stickley Brothers Company in Grand Rapids, Michigan, not to be confused with the since-dissolved 1886 New York–based company of the same name. (Grand Rapids was home to more than 40 furniture firms in 1900.) Their furniture design was marketed as "Quaint" or "Arts and Crafts," and it looked very like brother Gustav's. In 1902 in Fayetteville, New York, Gustav's other brothers Leopold and J. George started a furniture line called "Handcraft," again with designs very like brother Gustav's. For a time they even used an L. & J. G. Stickley symbol that looked like Gustav's medieval joiner's compass. Other trade names popular at the time—and surely designed to lure buyers into thinking they were Gustav Stickley's Craftsman originals—were "Craftsman: Mission," "Crafts-Style," "Cloister Style Life-Time Furniture" and "Limbert's Holland Dutch Arts and Crafts." Besides this competition, in later years (1912-13) the Come-Packt Furniture Company and even Sears and Roebuck got into the act of selling Mission furniture. You can imagine how Stickley felt about this. After half a lifetime of getting his designs refined, and after working so hard to popularize them, he saw knock-offs (many made by his own brothers!), some mass-produced by machines and sold through catalogs, cutting into a business he'd built on the premise of visionary, anti-urban philosophers who aspired to a medieval guild ideal.

But Gustav Stickley held on and flourished still. He appeared in the 1906 *Who's Who*, and earned enough profit and stature to be associated with the New York Athletic Club, the Engineer's Club, the National Arts Club and the Society of Craftsmen. He also fearlessly experimented with designs, and even started working on a larger scale. Like the architects he admired, Stickley began advocating interior design themes or "total environments" as a natural outgrowth of his furniture designs. "I saw that the way a man's house was planned and built had as much influence upon his family's health and happiness as had the furniture they lived with," Stickley wrote. "Besides, such unassuming furnishings as mine were out of place in elaborate overornamented interiors. They needed the sort of rooms and woodwork and exterior that would be in keeping with their own homelike qualities. They suggested, by their sturdy build and friendly finish, an equally sturdy and friendly type of architecture. This being the case, why not build homes that would be in sympathy with the Craftsman ideal? Thus evolved what has since come to be known as Craftsman architecture."

Stickley's architecture business was launched, and in 1902, he started offering through his magazine details for "The Craftsman House." In 1903 Stickley was first listed in the Syracuse city directory as an architect. While Stickley was beginning

> *"The love you liberate in your work is the love you keep."*
>
> DOOR CARVING, ROYCROFT SALON, ROYCROFT INN, EAST AURORA, NEW YORK (1903)

to push into the area of architecture and home plans, he was also pushing the designs of his furniture, improving, tweaking and adjusting proportions to get them exactly to his liking. Then in June 1903, Stickley hired an eccentric designer named Harvey Ellis. He would stay with Stickley until Ellis's death seven months later. But in that short time, this brilliant, reportedly alcoholic, design genius pushed Stickley in a direction he may not have gone alone, by making Stickley's furniture designs more graceful. He also brought to *The Craftsman* his supreme illustrating skills, as he illustrated his own as well as Stickley's whole-house Craftsman designs.

Like Stickley, Ellis was predisposed to use natural materials, and—echoing a Japanese influence that Stickley had revealed in earlier magazine articles in *The Craftsman*—Ellis brought kindred oriental influences to the design work he did on Stickley's behalf. Ellis's designs can be found in a wide range of Stickley Craftsman products during this time, from Stickley's fabrics to the house designs that appeared in *The Craftsman*.

Perhaps of most interest to the historians of Stickley's furniture, Ellis brought a lightness and elegance to the design, with thinner, less primitive-looking lines. He muted the medieval features that had been seen to date. Ellis introduced curves, like the ones seen in the underside of the bookcase and coffee table presented in this book (see pages 87 and 94, respectively), and his influence can also be seen in the delicate air rendered by the slender, closely grouped slats in the coffee table. Whereas the couch design included here is a quintessential "early" Stickley Mission piece (see page 124), with thick poke-through tenons, substantial slats and timber-like cross rails, the Ellis influence brought to Stickley an ornamental flavor. In Ellis's whole-house designs, featured in *The Craftsman*, you can see the influence of the architects C. F. A. Voysey and especially of Charles Rennie Macintosh. The transformation that Ellis brought is remarkable, and can

Fig. 5 *Harvey Ellis, who worked briefly for Stickley from 1903 to 1904, brought lightness and grace to Stickley's designs (right). The Eastwood chair (left), made just three years earlier, is primitive by comparison and shows how dramatically Stickley's designs evolved.*

easily be seen by comparing a chair made in 1901 to one made in 1904 (see Fig. 5, left and right, respectively). The early chair has a medieval thickness and heaviness with poke-through tenons on the arms. Ellis's creation has narrower legs, elegant inlaid back slats and thinner arms.

Ellis died at the age of 52, and was eulogized by Stickley as "a man of unusual gifts; possessing an accurate and exquisite sense of color, a great facility in design and a sound judgment of effect.... Altogether, he is to be regretted as one who possessed the sacred fire of genius." Ellis's access to the pure design spirit was so powerful that some draftsmen, it is reported, used to nick the edges of their T-square to mimic Ellis's wavy lines (lines made wavy by Ellis's nervous condition), in much the same way aspiring poets of the era would propagate a consumptive look, under the false assumption that creative people were more prone to the disease.

As anyone even vaguely familiar with Gustav Stickley's life can attest, his downfall and bankruptcy in 1916 came as a result of overambition, rather than from sloth or hubris. When Stickley's empire was at its peak, his Craftsman Workshops, like Morris's and like the medieval guilds Stickley saw as his ideal, were producing not only a wide variety of furniture, but fabrics and rugs too. He had more than 50 Craftsman outlet franchises nationwide, a growing Stickley Homebuilders Club, a Craftsman Contracting Company (which flourished only briefly) and sawmills and land holdings in the Adirondacks, where he milled the wood required for his products.

Even with these flourishing successes, Stickley still had not achieved his grandest vision. In 1908 he bought 600 acres in Morris Plains, New Jersey, where he planned to build the Craftsman Farms, a living compound, educational center, school for boys and meeting place that would work hand in glove with his Manhattan showcase interests, which he'd established in 1905 and planned to expand. Stickley's original plans for the Morris Plains site, only partially realized, included a main house for meetings, a number of home sites, guest cottages and a farm for growing crops and raising livestock. His Manhattan plans, which he realized but which drove him to bankruptcy, principally included the Craftsman Building, located at 6 East 39th Street. This 12-story building would include showrooms for furniture, draperies, rugs and interior decorating, as well as workshops, his magazine's editorial offices, a library and a top-floor restaurant, which would be furnished with food brought in from his farms in nearby Morris Plains (see Fig. 6).

But just as Stickley was planning his most grandiose and consummate achievements (1912-13), his businesses were beginning to fail, partially due to the competition, partially due to changing tastes and partially because Stickley didn't introduce many new furniture designs around this time, in the belief that he had perfected them beyond improvement. And truth be told, even in the best of times, the Craftsman Building he was erecting in New York was very expensive and by anyone's judgment shouldn't have been built, especially given Stickley's dwindling cash flow. Indeed, Stickley's business manager son-in-law, Ben Wiles, advised against it and eventually resigned in protest of Stickley's foolish perseverance.

In March 1915, just two years after the Craftsman Building opened, Gustav Stickley declared bankruptcy. What remained of his once-mighty Craftsman empire were the magazine, *The Craftsman*, which continued publication through December 1916, and the Craftsman Farms. *The Craftsman* soon merged with *Art World*, and lost any connection with Stickley. The buildings at Craftsman Farms, including a main house—Stickley's family residence—and some farm outbuildings, were sold in 1918 to the Farney family, the same year Stick-

Fig. 6 *Stickley's Craftsman Building contained a slice of every aspect of his empire when it opened in 1913, from showrooms and workshops to a top-floor restaurant. Unfortunately, it drove him to bankruptcy.*

ley's wife, Eda, died of a stroke. Gustav's brothers Leopold and J. George bought Gustav's Eastwood factory and the rights to his name and designs.

As for changing public tastes, L. & J. G. Stickley continued to produce Craftsman-style furniture in Eastwood until nearly the end of the next decade. Around 1927, responding to the consumer's desire for Colonial reproductions, L. & J. G. Stickley began making the Cherry Valley line of furniture.

After 1918, Gustav Stickley worked for a time at a mattress company in Wisconsin, and then for his brothers Leopold and George, but he eventually lost his taste for the business and retired to the home of his daughter Barbara and son-in-law Ben Wiles in Syracuse, New York. This was the home where he had once before lived, a home whose interior design served as a watershed event in his life, as it was here that he put in place his whole-house, unified Craftsman style, after a fire had gutted it years earlier.

For the next 24 years it seems he mostly tinkered with inventing new wood finishes (his daughter recalls having to call the plumber often to remove pipes clogged with varnish). And he fulfilled his grandfatherly duties by teaching Barbara's children. He dabbled some in design, planning the Village Waterworks of Skaneateles, New York, and oversaw the building of a log cabin for the Wileses on Lake Skaneateles.

Gustav Stickley died April 20, 1942. He was 85 years old.

The interest in Mission and Craftsman furniture had waned by the early 1920s. With World War I over, soldiers returned home from Europe with changing tastes. The more adventurous sought out Art Deco, and the more traditional opted for Colonial reproductions. Mission furniture was relegated to second-class status, and was even considered furniture for camps and secondary living areas for many years, as Modernism became the dominant style and held sway until well into the 1960s.

Then something remarkable happened. In 1972, Princeton University held a milestone exhibit, "The Arts and Crafts Movement in America: 1876-1916." A resurgence of interest had started. Perhaps as a replay of the backlash against the Industrial Revolution, this time played out against the Information Revolution, collectors started hankering for the well-made, honest furniture of the Arts and Crafts period. Stickley's work and all things Mission started becoming fashionable, and the fires of that interest quickly flared to a blaze. In a famous 1988 event that marks the high point of the resurgence of the Mission movement, movie star Barbra Streisand paid $363,000 at an auction for a 1903 sideboard that Gustav Stickley

had designed for his Syracuse, New York, house. Another bidder gave $16,500 for an Arts and Crafts vase that had a hole drilled in the bottom for a lamp cord. In that same week, a Gustav Stickley dining room table sold for $44,000, and a Gustav Stickley couch went for for $19,800.

Since 1988, prices have dropped somewhat, though authentic, period Gustav Stickley or L. & J. G. Stickley furniture is indeed valuable, especially when in good condition (or restorable) and stamped (or "signed") with the shop's symbol. But values are unpredictable. At a recent auction in rural Maine, a stamped Stickley-Simmonds chair—damaged, crudely repaired and in need of work—sold for $125, accompanied by complaints from the local dealers that the price was "surprisingly high." That same day, in a cluttered antique store, two "very clean," stamped Stickley chairs were offered for $500 each, and an unstamped Stickley rocker in very good condition went for $95.

The fact that the prices are unpredictable and all over the map reflects the current market for Mission antiques. The pieces are scattered far and wide. Multipiece sets have been broken up. Lineage is unclear. Many of the finishes are often not original, or have been treated with modern stains. Some of the furniture has been painted. The same piece purchased at an estate sale in Maine for $100 may go for $500 at an upscale Soho gallery in New York. The Stickley chairs at the dealer's in Maine, who has perhaps heard of the prices Stickley gets at city auctions and is convinced he is sitting on a gold mine, may sell for only $150 in the best of times. If you enter the speculative antiques market, prepare yourself. Read a wide variety of journals and books on the period, and carefully watch relative prices in galleries, antique stores and auctions. Of course, instead of buying Mission furniture in a risky market, you can, as this book proposes, simply make it yourself.

CHAPTER I

Getting Ready

Wood Choice & Prep

Original Mission furniture used white oak, and that's what is recommended for the projects in this book. White oak, which is tan or light brown, is a superior wood because it is nearly waterproof. That is why it's used in ships and barrels. White oak is resistant to rot and decay for two reasons. First, the annual growth rings are very compact, so the wood is tight and dense, and not prone to admit water. Second, the pores of white oak are filled with mineral deposits called *tyloses*, which seal out water and dirt. In addition to these wonderful natural virtues, there is another reason oak has been used for generations to make furniture: It is beautiful. The grain lines of white oak have a glorious look when milled for furniture.

Red oak, which is not as tightly grained as white oak, has fewer tyloses sealing its pores, and therefore is more apt to rot or decay. It is distinctly reddish in color and, like white oak, is attractive when milled for furniture stock. For the projects presented in this book, though, it's best to use white oak, as it's the authentic lumber stock used by the Mission masters.

Among hardwoods, oak is one of the strongest and most durable. In fact, one of the reasons antique Mission furniture has endured and remained

so valuable is because of the durability of the wood from which it's made. But another reason is the distinct look that white oak stock has when it is finished and treated in the Mission style. The rich, dark hues typical of Mission furniture were obtained precisely because of the way white oak took on stains or reacted to "fuming," a finishing treatment that darkens the natural tannin contained in oak through exposure to ammonia fumes (see pages 47-50). Even with the trickery of modern stains and finishes, you can get only a pale imitation of the traditional Mission look using other woods such as pine, ash or maple (although some Mission furniture was built with cherry).

When you purchase oak (or any wood), you have choices in species, milling types, moisture content, grade and finish, all of which affect the appearance of the finished product and the price.

Plainsawn & Quartersawn Lumber

Depending on the wood-milling process, all lumber, hardwood or softwood, is either "plainsawn" or "quartersawn." With plainsawn lumber (see Fig.1A), the circular growth rings of a log are at 45 degrees or less to the flat surface of the milled board. (This kind of milling is also called "tangential cut.") Most lumber today is plainsawn, because it makes the most of the wood available in each log, and this milling technique produces the widest boards.

For quartersawn milling, the log is first cut in lengthwise quarters, then boards are cut out of each quarter of the log (see Fig. 1B). This milling process creates narrower boards, but the grain patterns are spectacular and very tight. Because the milling of quartersawn lumber is more labor intensive and more wasteful than the milling of plainsawn lumber, quartersawn boards are more expensive than plainsawn boards.

The tighter the grain pattern in a board, the more stable the wood. This is because the growth rings are the part of the wood most apt to expand and contract, as they respond to the loss of water through the drying process or the absorption of water in the air. In plainsawn boards, the growth rings are exposed and broad relative to the surface area of the board, enabling the board to change size dimensionally as the growth rings expand and contract. This can cause cupping, warping, twisting and splitting. Since quartersawn wood has a tighter grain pattern, with a smaller section of the growth rings exposed, there is less chance for dimensional changes in the wood.

The only two drawbacks of quartersawn wood are that it is hard to get (often you have to special-order it) and it is expensive.

Moisture Content

Wood should have approximately the same relative moisture content as the air around it. If the wood has a higher moisture content than the ambient air, it will shrink as it loses water. Such shrinkage will loosen joints and open up cracks where one piece of wood joins another. On the other hand, if the wood is too dry, it will swell as it absorbs water, causing damage to joints.

Newly cut wood has a high moisture content, and it is dried in one of two ways: air-dried or kiln-dried. Air-dried wood doesn't cost the sawmill much to process, because the boards are just set out in the open air until their moisture content matches the air's

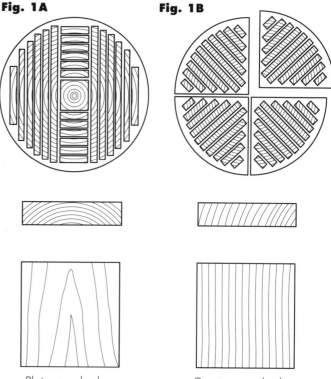

Fig. 1A | **Fig. 1B**

Plainsawn lumber | Quartersawn lumber

Fig. 1A *Most lumber is plainsawn. It is less dimensionally stable than quartersawn, but also less expensive. With plainsawn lumber, the circular growth rings of a log are at 45 degrees or less to the flat surface of the milled board. Plainsawn boards have broad, exposed growth rings, and the board can change size dimensionally as the growth rings expand and contract, leading to cupping, warping, twisting and splitting.*

Fig. 1B *Quartersawn logs are first cut lengthwise in quarters. Then boards are cut from each quarter. This milling process creates narrow boards with spectacular grain patterns. Because quartersawn boards have tighter growth rings, they are less likely to change dimensionally than are plainsawn boards.*

moisture content. Wood that is actively dried in a kiln is called kiln-dried and is stamped KD. Many premium woods, hardwoods and softwoods alike, are kiln-dried, which drives up the wood's cost, but you are assured a more stable product.

Lumber is sold with a moisture content of 15%

to 19%. Wood used in furniture should be between 6% and 12%, so even kiln-dried wood should be "seasoned" in the area where it eventually will be used, to allow its moisture content to match that of the air around it. For example, hardwood flooring, such as oak, must be stored at the construction site until it adapts to the ambient air. Only then is it ready to be installed. Likewise, lumber used to make Mission furniture should be stored in a clean, very dry interior location so the wood can stabilize.

Lumber Grades

Hardwood is graded for appearance and strength. There are four grades: FAS for "first and second," followed by No. 1 common, No. 2 common and No. 3 common.

It takes a lot of work to make No. 2 and No. 3 common grades suitable for furniture. You'll have to over-order the quantity you actually need and then cut out defects before getting good, usable knot-free wood. No. 1 common lumber is of adequate quality, but for the best hardwood, FAS grade is the premium choice.

Within the FAS grade there are other subcategories. "Clear select FAS" means the wood is knot-free, while "FAS with one clear side," means only one side of the wood is knot-free. For the projects in this book, you'll need clear select FAS.

On the lumberyard's list of available woods, you may see the designation S2S or S4S, meaning "sanded two sides" or "sanded four sides." (Sometimes this is written as D4S; the "D" stands for "dressed.") All of the terms simply indicate the number of sides of the board that are finished—planed and sanded. Boards with an S2S designation will have rough edges and two sides finished; S4S lumber will have all the edges and sides finished. For the furniture in this book, the ideal choice is S4S, because all sides of the wood will be exposed, even after the furniture is assembled, and you don't want a rough appearance from any vantage point.

If you are buying hardwood directly from a sawmill, you may have to finish the wood yourself. This takes time but will save you money. First, pass the wood through a planer until you have the desired finish on both faces of the board. Next, square up the edges by running the boards through a table saw. Then scrape and sand the wood to a desirable smoothness (see pages 23-25 for instructions).

When buying lumber, don't hesitate to be picky. Refuse boards that you are unhappy with or that have even a small defect. You're not required to accept the wood that a mill or lumberyard pulls from the stacks. In fact, you can ask to search through the stacks on your own for lumber that you deem suitable.

You'll find, however, that even clear FAS oak occasionally may have small knots or imperfections ("wanes"), as the grading system allows for some of this. But for your Mission furniture, you don't want any knots to show. If there are knots in the lumber you are given, either refuse it or be sure you can position the knots so they are out of sight in the finished product.

Nominal vs. Actual Board Dimensions

When you buy an oak 2x4, you may expect to get a piece of lumber 2 inches high by 4 inches wide. But if you measure it, you'll find that the wood is often thinner and narrower than that; it's actually closer to 1½ inches by 3½ inches. This is because lumber has "nominal" dimensions and "actual" dimensions. The nominal dimension is the size of the wood before final milling and shrinkage. The actual dimension is predictably smaller. Likewise, a 1x2 is actually ¾ inch by 1½ inches. Although the difference between actual and nominal dimensions in hardwoods is less than in framing lumber, be aware that the dimension you order ("nominal") will not always be the dimension you end up with ("actual").

Note: When purchasing lumber using the cut list included with each project in this book, remember that this list is based on actual, not nominal, sizes. When the Cut List and Materials calls for a board of a certain length and width, chances are you will have to get a larger board and mill it to the proper dimensions with your table saw and chop saw.

Board Feet

Hardwood lumber is often sold by "board feet." This is different from buying shelf board pine or 2x4s for doing odd jobs around the house. Those pieces of lumber are sold at unit prices. An 8-foot 2x4 may be priced at $3.00, or a 4-foot 1x8 at $2.40. But hardwood is sold by calculating how many board feet are contained in the piece of lumber you are buying. A board foot is a board 1 inch thick by 12 inches by 12 inches (1x12x12 inches), or the equivalent of those dimensions. For example, a 1-inch-thick board 6 inches wide by 24 inches long is one board foot. No matter what the dimensions are on the board you buy, a board foot is 144 cubic inches, and can be figured with the formula below, where T = thickness, W = width and L = length.

$$\frac{T \text{x} W \text{x} L}{12} = board\ feet$$

By calculating the board feet for your Mission furniture project, you can call your local hardwood supplier and get a pretty good idea of the overall cost of your lumber by asking for the supplier's board-foot costs.

Preparing the Wood

Though oak is a very stable wood, it's a good idea, as suggested earlier, to dry it out once you get it into your shop. Stack it in a protected, dry area, with dry scrap wood between the stacks to allow air to flow through and around the stock.

It's easy to convince yourself to just start building the furniture before sanding all the stock. It's

tempting, too, because the S4S wood looks pretty darn finished when it arrives. But don't be fooled: It *still* needs to be sanded. And once the various pieces of furniture are assembled, it is very difficult to get in all the nooks and joints to sand them smooth. So even before cutting your wood for the various projects in this book, sand it first as described below.

Sanding

You'll be doing lots of sanding, both before and after assembly, so buy, borrow or rent an electric sander. Hand sanding is extremely hard work, and even though some people may claim that it "brings you closer to the wood," nothing compares with the dramatic efficiency of planers and electric palm and belt sanders.

A palm sander is an ideal, essential sanding tool (see Fig. 2). It is lightweight and easy to manipulate, and can be loaded with any grade of sandpaper called for in our projects, from coarse (80 grit) to fine (220 grit).

A belt sander is also handy. When loaded with

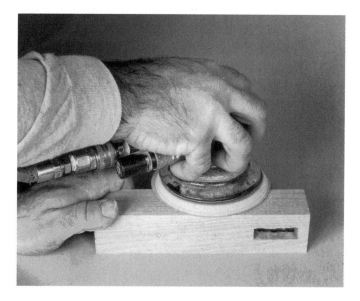

Fig. 2 *A palm sander can accommodate a variety of grades of sandpaper, from coarse to fine. The one shown here is pneumatic, but inexpensive electric models are equally effective.*

Fig. 3 *Before the final sanding, scrape your wood by holding a steel wood scraper at a slight angle to the stock surface, and pulling it toward you.*

80-grit paper, it can quickly take down rough wood. This may be an essential step to preparing your wood, depending on the quality of the milling or if it was sanded or planed at the mill. In any event, a belt sander is great for a first pass over rough spots or to take down any milling or saw blade marks. But be careful. If you use a belt sander, experiment on some scrap wood until you get a feel for this unwieldy tool. The slightest mistake with a belt sander can gouge wood, or take it down unevenly where the sander lingers too long.

The most important aspect of sanding is choosing the proper kind and grit of sandpaper. For early sanding, when the wood is still rough, use 80- and 120-grit sandpaper to start and 180- and 220-grit sandpaper to finish. Optimally, get garnet sandpaper, which is the reddish brown or amber-colored sandpaper (not the black or deep blue kind). Garnet gives the softest finish because the tiny garnet sanding grits are blocky and attached to the paper backing with an animal hide glue that softens with the friction heat generated when you sand. If you can't

find garnet, use aluminum oxide sandpaper. Avoid silicon carbide or aluminum zirconia, which are for rough finishes and solid-surfacing.

Before cutting your wood to length, be sure to do a thorough initial pass with 80- and 120-grit sandpaper. This will take the wood down to a smooth finish. Then "scrape" the wood. Using a steel wood scraper (a woodworking tool available at most supply houses), and holding it at 80 degrees to the stock surface, pull it toward you at a slight bias (nearly square) to the grain (see Fig. 3). When scraped wood is sanded with finer-grit sandpapers, the resulting finish is silky smooth.

After your stock has been sanded, scraped, sanded again and cut to length, touch sand it all with 120-grit paper to smooth out any saw blade "tear-outs." (Tear-outs occur when the saw blade rips up pieces of the board's face as it starts and finishes the cut.) Then change to 180-grit sandpaper, and after that, 220-grit sandpaper.

Since the palm sander oscillates, it is hard to "sand with the grain," which is required for the final sanding. (Some palm sanders leave swirl marks in the wood that show up only after finishes are applied.) So when you are ready to do the final sanding (with 220-grit paper), you may want to set down the palm sander and use either a sanding block (sandpaper wrapped around a 2x4 or a piece of plastic designed for this specific use), or sandpaper simply folded in quarters. Remember also to sand with the grain, not across it.

Here's something else to keep in mind when planning your sanding strategy. After the furniture is assembled, you will need to sand it yet again with 220-grit sandpaper. But you may find that you can't get into the far reaches or corners of your joints. For these areas, you'll want to use a detail sander. This tool, which costs around $80, has a triangular-shaped head that can get in most anywhere. Adhesive-backed sandpaper (up to 240 grit) can be attached to the sander head. Use a finer-grit paper for this round of sanding. Don't expect dramatic results, though. The head vibrates almost imperceptibly, and it only works well when sanding already smooth wood.

Tools

A few specialized woodworking tools, as well as the more standard ones, are required for the Mission furniture projects in this book. If you have a workshop filled with state-of-the art equipment, that's great, but for those who don't, this chapter explains how you can make the more difficult tasks easier and the final product as professional-looking as possible.

If you are just getting started in woodworking, and you don't want to buy the more expensive equipment described here, you can always precisely mark your wood and hire a nearby woodworking shop to make the cuts or borings for you. As you work with various tools, some very sophisticated, keep in mind that Stickley didn't have the benefit of highly engineered tools. His craftsmanship had to take up where the early woodworking machines left off. It's a humbling thought.

Hand Tools

The standard carpenter's tools you'll need include a hammer, rubber-headed mallet, Phillips and slot-head screwdrivers, a handsaw and a hand plane. Add to this assortment a small backsaw (also called a dovetail saw or tenon saw). We will use this small handsaw to flush-cut pegs and plugs that hide recessed screw heads (see page 39, Fig. 19).

You'll also want a set of wood chisels. If your chisels aren't razor sharp, send them out for sharpening or sharpen them yourself with a whetstone, so that you can get clean cuts. A dull chisel is worthless: It can do more damage than good. Plus, it is unsafe because it won't perform as expected and you may end up compensating for the chisel's dullness with force, which can lead to dangerous slippage of the chisel.

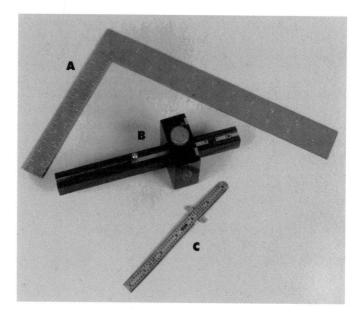

Fig. 4 *Common measuring and marking tools: a small steel square* (A), *a marking gauge* (B) *and a steel ruler with sliding collar* (C).

Marking Tools. All quality woodworking calls for precision cuts and accurate boring. But before you can make any cut or drill any hole, you have to mark it precisely. To get off to a good start, be sure to have a generous collection of sharp No. 2 pencils on hand. (Keep them sharp with a razor utility knife.) Avoid the thick, flat carpenter's pencils or crayons; the lines they make are too thick and inaccurate.

You may also want a scratch awl for scoring cut lines. By scoring the board's face along the cut line, you create a crease in the wood that prevents tearouts, and the result is a cleaner cut. (By analogy, think of how much more easily and cleanly paper rips along a crease line after it has been folded. The same is true of wood.)

A small steel square (see Fig. 4A) or combination square is essential for making square cut lines, and a marking gauge (see Fig. 4B) is required for scoring cut lines along boards. A marking gauge is really a scratch awl mounted on a jig. It has an oval head that you set against the edge of a board. A small square wooden arm slides through the head and can be adjusted for length. The arm has a metal point on its underside. When you place the head on a board edge and then slide it, the metal point on the underside of the arm scores a cut line wherever you set it. This tool is essential for marking mortise-and-tenon cut lines.

A small ruler is also useful, and the best kind has a center section that slides out, or a sliding collar, for exact measurements (see Fig. 4C). This tool is indispensable for accurately measuring the tenon lengths on many of the projects presented here.

You'll need a doweling jig as well. This is a hand tool designed to center and precisely position dowel holes (see page 41, Fig. 24).

Clamps. Nearly all of the projects presented in this book require clamping. There are numerous varieties of clamps available, and since they are generally inexpensive, it is wise to have a number of them available.

Pipe clamps (see Fig. 5A) and sliding bar clamps (see Figs. 5C and 5D) are ideal for drawing together pieces of wood and holding them in place after applying glue and waiting for it to dry. Both types of clamps work on the same principle:

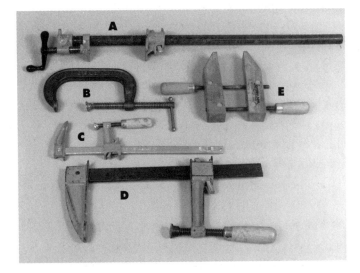

Fig. 5 *Some clamps to keep handy: a pipe clamp* (A), *a C-clamp* (B), *a small bar clamp* (C), *a large bar clamp* (D) *and a hand-screw clamp* (E).

At one end of the bar or pipe is a fixed "stop." At the other end is a movable stop with a threaded rod attached that works like a one-way valve. You can slide the stop in one direction, yet it will bite against the bar or pipe if pressure is applied. When you want to clamp two pieces of wood together, you slide the movable stops until they are snug against the joint, and then crank down on the thread rod for additional pressure. Some woodworkers prefer pipe clamps over bar clamps, because bar clamps tend to flex and bend under pressure, whereas the pipe clamp is unyielding. Almost all of the projects in this book call for pipe or bar clamps.

Standard C-clamps (see Fig. 5B) are also very handy, though they don't have the range and extension that bar or pipe clamps have. Nonetheless, they are useful for holding together joints and shorter pieces of wood.

Hardwood hand-screw wood clamps (often called Jorgensens, after their manufacturer) consist of hardwood tongues held together with two threaded metal rods (see Fig. 5E). As you turn the metal rods in opposite directions (using wood handles mounted on the rods), the clamps tighten. Since the clamps are made of wood, they tend to do less damage to furniture stock. Hand-screw clamps come in very handy in furniture work.

Another type of clamp that is popular these days is a "quick clamp," which can be worked with only one hand. Quick clamps have a trigger handle (like a caulk gun), which you simply squeeze to draw the clamp jaws together.

Finally, you might have use for corner clamps. These clamps hold wood at a precise 90-degree angle. They are sometimes called picture-frame clamps because most people use them for making the corners on frames.

Power Tools

Saws. A chop saw loaded with a "finish" or "combo" blade is the ideal tool for cutting boards to the proper length or for cutting angles. You can make square and angled cuts on a table saw, but unless you are proficient with a guide, you may get imprecise cut lines. So if you have access to a chop saw, use it.

Any good table saw (see page 36, Fig. 8) loaded with an 80-tooth ATB (alternate tooth bevel) blade will work for most of the projects presented here, but the saw must have a miter gauge. The miter gauge acts as a guide that allows you to maintain a consistent square or angle cut as you push the wood through the saw. As you will see when you get into the joinery chapter of this book, the table saw will be essential for making tenons and ripping stock edges at an angle.

For cutting the rounded aspects of Mission furniture or scribing the arms on the Morris chair, you will need a jigsaw or saber saw. Of course, if you have a full-blown workshop, then a band saw will do just as well (see page 46, Fig. 37). The jigsaw or saber saw can easily cut curves because their blades are very thin and they don't bind when following curved lines. Use a finish blade in your jigsaw or saber saw. It has a greater number of teeth per inch than a rough blade, and it makes a smoother cut.

Drills. A variable-speed drill is an essential and versatile tool that will be used frequently in this book. The best kind is a cordless drill, because you are unencumbered by electric cords and can move freely. Be sure to keep two batteries on hand for your drill, one to use and one to charge. When the one you are using is drained, swap it for the one that's been charging.

There are three kinds of holes that will be used in the projects that follow: predrilled, countersunk and dowel holes.

Predrilled holes: The wedge action of a screw will split hardwood if it is not predrilled with a pilot hole, so be sure to drill pilot holes for all your screws. To predrill pilot holes, use a standard wood drill bit, and drill down three-quarters the length of the screw. If you have a 2½-inch screw, drill a pilot hole 1⅞ inches deep. To make sure you don't overdrill, mark the 1⅞-inch depth on the drill bit with a band of masking tape. Drill down until the masking tape touches the face of the board. (Woodworking supply stores also sell drill bit rings for marking bits for this purpose.)

If a pilot hole is oversized, the screw won't grab the wood securely and may tear out when the joint comes under stress. Use the table below to determine pilot hole bit sizes. The drill size is labeled on the case the bits come in; the screw gauge is on the box.

Screw Gauge	Pilot Hole Diameter
#3	1/16 inch
#4	1/16 inch
#5	5/64 inch
#6	5/64 inch
#7	3/32 inch
#8	3/32 inch
#9	7/64 inch
#10	7/64 inch

Countersunk holes: A countersunk hole requires a simple drilling and screwing method that buries the screw head below the surface of a board so it can be covered with a wood plug or hidden from view (see Fig. 6). There is a specially designed drill bit for just this task called a countersink bit, which has both a long, thin drill bit to create the pilot hole and a stubby bit to cut a recess for the screw head. Typically, this recess is about ¼ inch deep. A countersink bit is set up to create the pilot hole and the countersunk hole in one smooth plunge of the drill.

Each countersink bit is designed to drill out for screws of a particular gauge. So, for #8 wood screws (the most common) you will use a #8 countersink (which happens to be a ⅜-inch countersink), a #7 screw uses a #7 countersink, and so on.

Dowel holes: For drilling holes to accommodate dowels, you first need to know the size of the

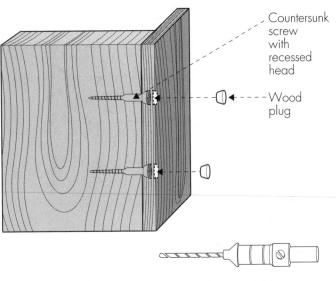

Countersunk screw with recessed head

Wood plug

Countersink bit

Fig. 6 *A countersink bit simultaneously drills two different-sized holes—one is a pilot hole for the screw and one is for a plug to cover the recessed screw head.*

dowel. Most of the dowels used in this book are ⅜ inch in diameter and 1½ inches long. No matter what the length, each dowel hole must accommodate half of the dowel's length plus an additional ¹⁄₁₆ inch so that the glue has someplace to go when the joint is squeezed by clamps. So, for a 1½-inch dowel, each hole will be ¾ inch plus ¹⁄₁₆ inch, or ¹³⁄₁₆ inch long.

When drilling for dowels, use a drill bit the same diameter as the dowel, never larger. Common dowel diameters are ¼, ⁵⁄₁₆, ⅜ and ½ inch, so use a corresponding drill bit of the same size. You can always double-check to see if the dowel and drill bit match by holding the base of the drill bit to the dowel. They should be the same diameter. The ultimate double check, of course, is that the dowel won't fit in a hole that is too small. (More on this in the joinery chapter.)

It is essential when drilling any hole to keep the drill perpendicular to the face of the board. If a pilot hole or dowel hole is askew, the screw and dowel will be askew, and the joint will not be square. Some newer drills have bubble levels built

into them so you can tell if you are entering the wood at an angle. This is a good feature to have. Otherwise, you have to eyeball it, or hold the tongue of a framing square up to the wood and use its body as a guide for your drill.

Electric Joinery Tools & Attachments. Some of the joinery used in authentic Mission furniture requires intermediate woodworking skills—skills you will learn in this book. Intermediate skills are a step above the plugged-screw or nailed-together woodworking you may have employed in previous woodworking projects, such as picnic tables, Adirondack chairs or bookshelves. Although an effort has been made to simplify the joinery here, you will need some electric joinery tools in addition to your table saw, chop saw and drill. These tools include a router or a mortising bit and mortising jig mounted on a drill press, a doweling jig and a plate joiner. For cutting tenons, a tenoning jig that fits on your table saw is the ideal tool, although a skilled woodworker could also accomplish this with a table saw alone.

Router: The common woodworking router is nothing more than a high-speed motor on which is

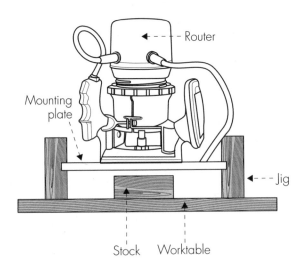

Router

Mounting plate

Jig

Stock   Worktable

Fig. 7 *When guided by a jig, a router can make precise cuts of varying configurations in wood stock. Be sure the work table, stock and jig are securely clamped or held fast before routing.*

Router Bits

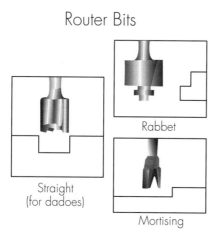

Straight
(for dadoes)

Rabbet

Mortising

Fig. 8 *A router cut's configuration depends on the router bit used. Here are some common router cuts and the bits that make them.*

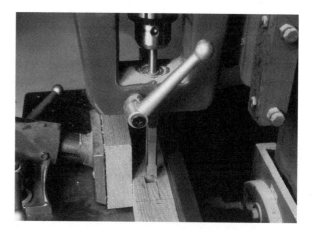

Fig. 10 *When mounted on a drill press, a mortising bit can drill a square hole. The square hole, or mortise, is what is required for a mortise-and-tenon joint.*

mounted a round sole plate (see Fig. 7). Different types of jigs, either mounted on the router or screwed in place to guide the router (called a mounting plate), keep the path of the router predictable.

The router can be loaded with a variety of router bits, each of which cuts a different kind of pattern into the wood (see Fig. 8). We will work with mainly one type of router bit in this book: a straight bit, which is not so much for making decorative patterns or edge treatments as for precisely cutting away wood to create joints or dadoes. (A dado is a groove or recess, typically larger than ¼ inch, cut in wood.)

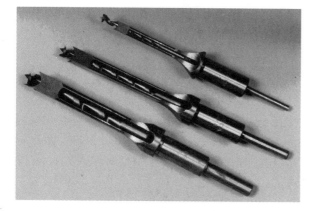

Fig. 9 *Mortising bits are essentially round drill bits run through a hollow, square chisel. They come in different sizes and must be mounted on a drill press.*

Drill press, mortising bit, mortising jig: For creating mortises, the ideal tool to use is a drill press. The drill press is loaded with two items: a mortising bit and a mortising jig. The bit cuts the wood as the jig holds it in place. A mortising bit is actually a tool that cuts a square hole (see Fig. 9). A standard drill bit is contained within a square hollow steel chisel. When it is plunged into the wood, the drill reams out most of the wood, and the chisel squares the sides. Since you can only cut relatively small squares with each plunge of the drill press, you need a device to hold the wood precisely for each plunge, yet move the wood squarely along for the next cut. That device is called a mortising jig. It is attached to the plate of the drill press, and it holds the wood in place as the bit plunges into it. As you turn a handle on the mortising jig, the wood moves squarely beneath the mortising bit, ensuring precise positioning (see Fig. 10).

If you don't have a drill press and a mortising jig to mount on it, you can make mortises with a router, albeit with some difficulty.

Tenoning jig: Although you can use a table saw and a router for cutting tenons, the work is far easier if you attach a tenoning jig to your table saw (see Fig. 11). A tenoning jig is a jig-and-clamp device that allows a piece of wood to be clamped

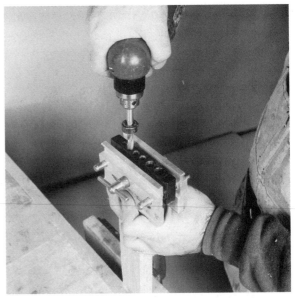

Fig. 11 *To cut a tenon, a tenoning jig helps maintain exact cut lines. As shown, oak stock is loaded in a jig and run through a table saw.*

Fig. 12 *To cut true dowel holes, square to the stock, a doweling jig maintains proper positioning of the drill bit.*

vertically and slid across the top of a table saw, square to the blade. It cuts clean, crisp "shoulders" for the tenons.

Doweling jig: This is a device (with varying size drill bit holes) that is clamped to the end or edge of a board (see Fig. 12). The jig allows you to precisely position your drill holes in the center of the board end or edge. If you were to try to cut these holes freehand, without a doweling jig, your dowel holes would probably not be square to the edge of the board, nor necessarily centered, and this would make the joint askew. This jig allows you to drill consistently centered, properly positioned holes in which you will insert dowels.

Plate joiner: Also called a biscuit joiner (see Fig. 13), a plate joiner is a tool that has a saw blade that plunges through a saw fence. The blade cuts reliefs in wood so that flat wood biscuits can be inserted. These wood biscuits help to join two pieces of wood together along their lengths.

Say, for example, that you need to join two 2-foot by 4-foot pieces of oak together edge to edge, for a tabletop. Simply gluing them along their

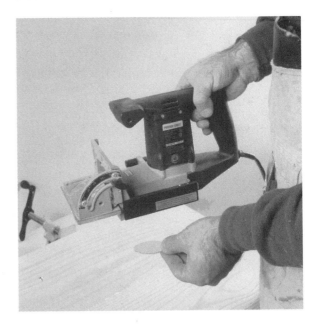

Fig. 13 *A biscuit joiner and biscuits are used to create a tight joint between boards. Biscuit joining is ideal for creating wide pieces of oak out of narrower ones, as required for tabletops or side panels.*

lengths might not create a strong enough bond. Instead, you will want to add biscuits, which act as splines, between the two pieces of wood. To do this, you not only have to cut saw blade-width openings along the length of the wood, but you have to position them precisely so the relief from one board precisely matches the relief cut in the opposing board and the splines (biscuits) will align. That's where the biscuit joiner comes in. After you have measured and marked where you want your biscuits to go, you position the fence of the biscuit joiner and pull the trigger. The blade starts to spin (like a table saw's blade). As you press the fence against the wood, the blade reveals itself, plunges through the fence, and makes a cut in the edge of the piece of wood. You do this same cut on the opposing piece of wood, and when they come together the cuts you've made will precisely line up. Then biscuits are glued and inserted into these relief cuts to join the boards together. (This joinery technique is covered in greater detail in the next chapter.)

Safety Precautions. Whenever you're working with power tools of any kind, it is important to take precautions. Never make any saw cut without eye and ear protection. Even a small particle in your eye can be very distracting and easily cause you to lose your concentration and thus your control over the tool in hand—not to mention the possible permanent eye damage you could incur. Always wear eye protection; use OSHA-approved or UL-listed safety glasses.

Though hearing loss is incremental, you can easily damage your ears with the noise these woodworking machines produce. Plus, the screaming noise of woodworking tools is distracting and aggravating, especially after a long day. Ear protection makes for a safer work environment, so get it and wear it.

Always eat a balanced diet when you are working around power tools. Eat regularly so your blood sugar doesn't drop, and don't load up on sugars or caffeine. You lose your concentration when you are tired or when your energy fades in long lapses between meals. Accidents seem to happen either early in the day or at the end of the day. Be careful, so you don't add to the accident statistics.

CHAPTER 2

Joinery

The most frequently used joint in Mission furniture is the mortise and tenon. The mortise is the "female" aspect of the joint, the slot into which the tenon is placed. The tenon is the "male" aspect, the tongue of wood inserted into the slot. There are two types of tenons. The first type, a "loose" or "slot" tenon, is a small piece of wood (sometimes rounded along its edges) that is inserted between two mortises. The second type, a "true tenon," is actually milled out of the lumber stock. The latter is what is used in all the Mission projects in this book.

Three kinds of mortise-and-tenon joints are used in Mission furniture: the blind mortise and tenon, where the tenon is entirely hidden in the mortise (see Fig. 1); the poke-through mortise and tenon, where the tenon protrudes all the way through the mortise and pokes through the other side, often with a chamfered cut to finish the end grain of the tenon (see Fig. 2); and the pegged

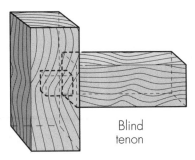

Fig. 1 *In a blind mortise-and-tenon joint, the tenon is hidden within the stock.*

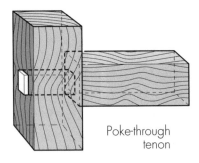

Fig. 2 *In a poke-through mortise-and-tenon joint, the mortise is cut all the way through the stock and the tenon protrudes out the other side.*

mortise and tenon, where the tenon (blind or poke-through) is held in the mortise with a peg (or pegs) driven perpendicular to it (see Fig. 3). These pegs are often small hand-cut pieces of hardwood, about as thick as a pencil.

The blind and poke-through tenons are cut using the same joinery principles and tools.

Shoulder-to-Shoulder Measurement

Before getting into the techniques for cutting these joints, you should understand the "shoulder-to-shoulder" principle of measuring tenoned stock and how it affects the furniture's dimensions. First, some definitions. The "shoulder" of a tenon is that part of the wood that extends up and down, perpendicular to the tongue of wood that is inserted into the mortise (see Fig. 5).

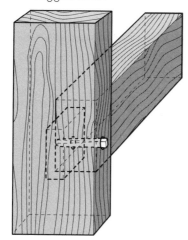

Pegged tenon

Fig. 3 *In a pegged tenon, hardwood pegs are used to hold the tenon in place.*

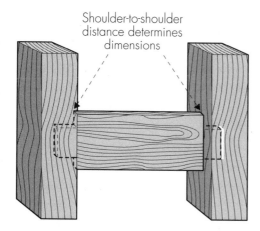

Shoulder-to-shoulder distance determines dimensions

Fig. 4 *Shoulder-to-shoulder distance is measured along the edge of the wood where it steps down to create the tenon's shoulder. This distance is the crucial measurement when making furniture, as it determines the actual distance between two pieces of wood.*

The tenon's shoulder should butt into the face of the mortised board and should sit square and tight against the board's face. The shoulder-to-shoulder distance establishes the dimension between those two mortised boards.

With blind mortise and tenons (where the tenon is buried out of sight and does not poke through the mortised board), the end-to-end dis-

tance of the tenons is not as crucial as the shoulder-to-shoulder distance of the wood stock. For blind mortise and tenons, as you trim your boards to get them to the right dimensions, you will be measuring and cutting from the shoulders, *not* from the ends of the tenons. If a tenon goes into a mortise and fits snug, but the shoulder does not come flush with the face of the board, your joint will be unstable and unsightly.

How big should a shoulder be? As a rule of thumb, the shoulder should be as high as the tenon is thick. If your tenon is 1 inch thick, make each shoulder 1 inch high.

Making a Mortise-and-Tenon Joint

No matter what kind of mortise and tenon you are going to use, they are all cut using the same principles. You cut out the mortise using a router or a mortising bit on a drill press; you cut the tenon using a table saw or a router. The following example, using a piece of wood actually measuring 2 inches by 4 inches, describes how to make a simple L-joint, comprised of a "rail" (horizontal piece of wood) and a "stile" (vertical piece of wood).

Marking the Joint

When laying out and cutting a mortise-and-tenon joint, the mortise should be the same size as the tenon that will fit into it. So the first step is to determine the tenon's dimensions. The tenon should be one-half of the end grain's surface area of the stock's actual dimension (see Fig. 5).

For our example, one-half of 2 inches is 1 inch, and one-half of 4 inches is 2 inches. Therefore, the tenon's dimensions are 1 inch by 2 inches. Note that its length is not yet known.

Once you know the tenon's width and height (1 inch by 2 inches), you can mark for the tenon on the end grain of the rail, and mark a correspond-

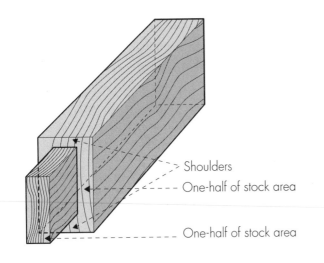

Fig. 5 *A tenon ideally should take up half the area of the stock. The shoulders of a tenon are the portions of wood above and below the tenon itself.*

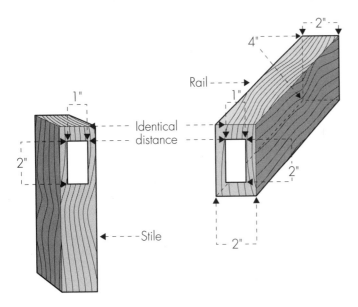
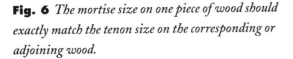

Fig. 6 *The mortise size on one piece of wood should exactly match the tenon size on the corresponding or adjoining wood.*

ing rectangle on the side of the stile stock, where the mortise will be cut (see Fig. 6). You will know where to position the mortise because its top line is 1 inch from the end of the stile, which is the height of the tenon's shoulder.

To mark one end of the mortise (the top end), set a marking gauge at 1 inch and slide it across the stock (see Fig. 7A). To mark the other (bottom) end of the mortise, add the shoulder height to the height of the tenon. In this case it is 1 inch plus 2 inches, or 3 inches. Set your marking gauge and slide it across the stock (see Fig. 7B).

With the top and bottom ends of the mortise marked, move to the side of the stock to mark the mortise's length. Reaching *across* the stock, set the marking gauge at 1½ inches (1 inch plus ½ inch), and slide the marking gauge up and down the stock to connect the mortise's top and bottom marks (see Fig. 7C). Then, set the marking gauge at ½ inch, and slide it up and down the stock in the same manner to connect the top and bottom marks on the other side of the mortise (see Fig. 7D).

You now have a rectangle that marks the outer edges of your mortise. And the marking gauge has scored the wood to ensure a clean cut with little or no tear-out.

Cutting the Mortise

Before cutting the mortise with a router or drill press, you have to know how deep to cut it. This measurement is ideally equal to the tenon's length (but for blind tenons, make the mortise a little longer than the tenon, say, 1/16 inch). Since the tenon should extend at least two-thirds of the way into the wood, for a piece of wood that is 2 inches by 4 inches, the mortise should be 2⅝ inches deep, plus 1/16 inch. Round it up to 2¾ inches.

If you are going to cut the mortise with a mortiser attached to your drill press, mark the mortising bit 2¾ inches up from the end with a band of masking tape so you know how far to plunge the bit into the wood. If you are using a router, set the bit height at 2¾ inches with your tape measure. Then, drill or rout out the 2¾-inch-deep mortise.

When you have finished routing or drilling out the mortise, clean the sides with a chisel and blow air into the mortise to remove all the wood chips.

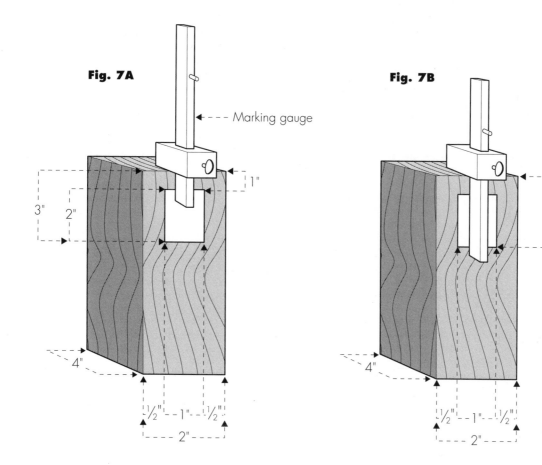

Fig. 7A

Marking gauge

1"

3" 2"

4"

½" — 1" — ½"

2"

Fig. 7B

3"

4"

½" — 1" — ½"

2"

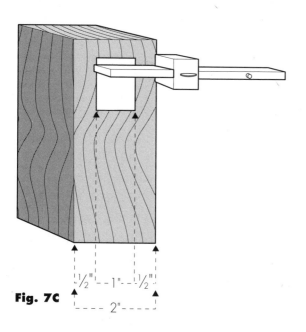

Fig. 7C

½" — 1" — ½"

2"

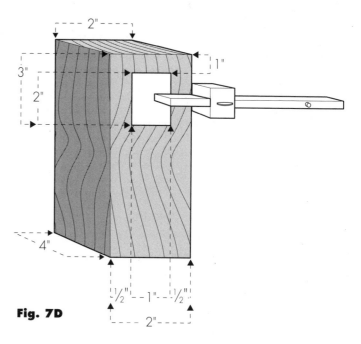

2"

3" 2"

1"

4"

½" — 1" — ½"

2"

Fig. 7D

Fig. 7A-D *Lay out your mortise dimensions, using a marking gauge set to the proper lengths.*

Fig. 8 *You can easily cut tenons with a table saw. With your marking gauge lines as guides, use a ruler to set the blade height.*

Fig. 9 *With the saw blade height set, run your stock through the table saw, and cut around the tenon on all four sides.*

Cutting the Tenon

When setting up to cut the tenon, you know its dimensions from the setup for cutting the mortise, but keep in mind the basic principle of sizing a tenon: The tenon should be at least half the end-grain area of the wood you are using. And as for tenon length, it should protrude entirely into the mortise, which should be bored two-thirds of the way through the stock. For example, a 2-inch by 4-inch piece of wood would have a 2¾-inch-long tenon, measuring 1 inch by 2 inches, inserted into a 2¾-inch mortise.

You can cut the tenon with a simple table saw, or for more control and ease, you can use a tenoning jig attached to your table saw (see page 30, Fig. 11). The advantage of a tenoning jig is that the jig uses a clamp system to hold the wood square and plumb to the table saw's blade. If you run the wood through the table saw without a jig, or with only a mitering guide, you need a sure eye and a *very* steady hand to make the shoulder cuts square.

For those using a table saw, the principle for cutting a tenon is very simple. Referring to the dimensions you determined for your wood, set the blade height (see Fig. 8) so it cuts into the wood and leaves the "true tenon" after cutting away excess all the way around the board.

Once you have your initial shoulder cuts made, you can do one of two things. You can either make repeated passes with your table saw to cut away to the true tenon (see Fig. 9), or you can rout out the wood using the initial cuts as your guide. Saw or rout on all four sides, and the true tenon will be revealed as you cut or rout away the wood (see Figs. 10 and 11).

Cutting Large Stock Mortises and Tenons

Cutting mortises on large stock lumber is relatively easy using a router or a drill press set up with a mortising bit. But if you plan to use a tenoning jig for cutting the tenon, you'll find that you can't load it with large stock. The jig is made for smaller stock lumber, and even if you could fit the wood into the jig, longer lengths of large stock would be impossible to manage because of their sheer weight. At least one of the projects presented in this book (the couch or "box settle," see page 124) requires that tenons be cut on large stock. Here's how to do it.

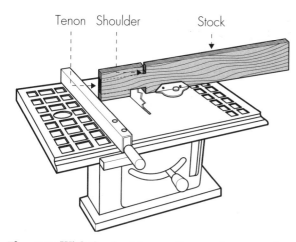

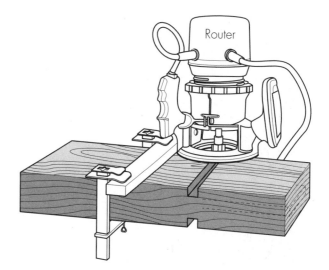

Fig. 10 *With the shoulders cut first, make repeated passes with the table saw to eat away the wood to create the tongue of the tenon.*

Fig. 11 *After a shoulder has been cut, you can use a router to cut away the wood to reveal the tongue of the tenon.*

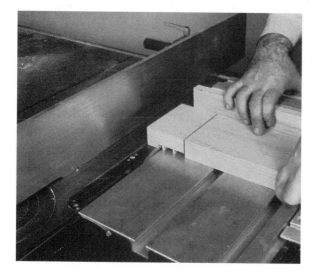

Fig. 12 *For cutting tenons in larger stock, make repeated passes with your table saw, but periodically leave some slivers of wood at the original height to serve as guides for your router.*

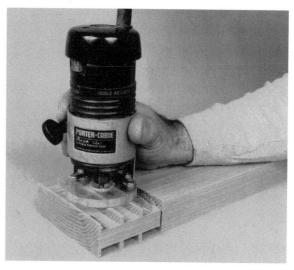

Fig. 13 *A router loaded with a straight bit is an ideal tool to use when cleaning up the sides of a tenon.*

First, mark for the tenon with a marking gauge using the method described earlier. Then run the wood through a table saw, but leave some slivers of wood at the original height (see Fig. 12). These will be routed or cut out later and will serve as guides (or "indexes") for your router when you clean up the tenon (see Fig. 13). After you have routed the tenon clean, chisel off the remaining sections of raised wood and use the same chisel to clean the tenon surface (see Fig. 14).

Test the joint by inserting just part of the tenon into the mortise. It should fit snug. If the tenon is too big, it can be sanded down. Be sure that you never force a tenon, because it will split or "blow out" the mortise, ruining all your painstaking work. (If the joint sticks together after you've tested it, separate the pieces by gently tapping them with a rubber mallet.)

Fig. 14 *After routing out the tenon, knock down and chisel away the remaining raised wood.*

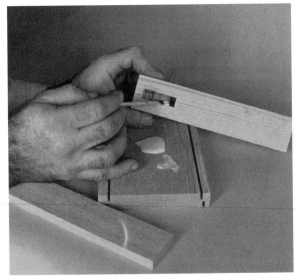

Fig. 15 *Use a brush to completely coat the walls of the mortise with carpenter's glue before inserting the tenon.*

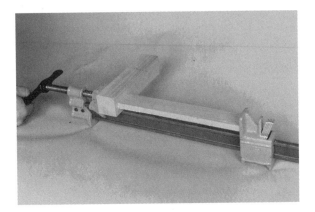

Fig. 16 *Once the joint is assembled, draw it tight and snug with a clamp.*

Fig. 17 *The pegs for a pegged mortise-and-tenon joint can be cut out of hardwood stock and trimmed with a utility knife.*

Gluing & Clamping

All mortise-and-tenon joints should be glued and clamped. Yellow carpenter's glue will serve perfectly well, as will specialty waterproof glues and epoxies that are on the market.

Apply the glue with an inexpensive, aluminum-handled bristle brush (called "suicide brushes" because you throw them away after each use). The brush will evenly distribute the glue and help prevent dry places inside the joint (see Fig. 15). Once the glue has been applied, fit the joint together and clamp it (see Fig. 16). You may want to insert blocks of scrap wood between the stock and the clamp to prevent the wood from being bruised by the clamp. If any glue squeezes out of the joint, clean it off with a rag before it has a chance to dry.

The Pegged Joint

If a project calls for pegged mortise-and-tenon joints, you need first to make some pegs. Using your table saw, "rip" some oak stock into ¼-inch by ¼-inch (or ⅜-inch by ⅜-inch) strips, approximately 12 to 18 inches long. ("Rip" is a term that describes the cutting technique of running wood stock through a table saw lengthwise, cutting parallel to the grain.) The resulting strips—and the pegs that will be made from them—will have grain running lengthwise.

Once you have some long strips, cut them into 1½-inch lengths, using a small handsaw. Then, with a very sharp knife or razor utility knife, cut chamfers and round one end; leave the other end square (see Fig. 17).

Next, mark and drill pilot holes for the pegs. The peg will be driven into the side of the mortised wood, through the tenon, and into the mortised wood on the other side of the tenon. If you are using just one peg, center the pilot hole so that when the peg is driven, it will protrude through the geometric center of the tenon. If you are using two pegs, symmetrically place them (see Fig. 18).

When choosing a drill bit for peg pilot holes, use the narrowest part of the peg to determine your drill bit size, and be careful about the depth of the hole. When fully driven in, the peg should protrude slightly above the face of the wood, so it can be neatly trimmed off. Above all, don't overdrill the peg holes because a recessed peg is unsightly. Drill into the joint, hammer in the pegs, and trim them with a backsaw (see Fig. 19). Clean up the pegs with a chisel (see Fig. 20), and sand them flush with the surface of the wood.

The Poke-Through Mortise and Tenon

The authentic Mission look often calls for poke-through tenons, where a mortise is drilled all the way through the wood, and the tenon protrudes through the mortise and out the other side (see Fig. 21). Calculating the tenon length is crucial, but easy to do. For poke-through tenons, the width of your wood (which equals the depth of the mortise) determines the initial tenon length, and anything you add to that tenon length will stick out the other side. A good poke-through standard length is ⅜ inch, but for pieces of wood smaller than 1 inch, try ¼ inch instead. Whatever poke-through length you use, be sure to add it to the initial tenon length. To get a sense of what the poke-through tenon will look like before the joint

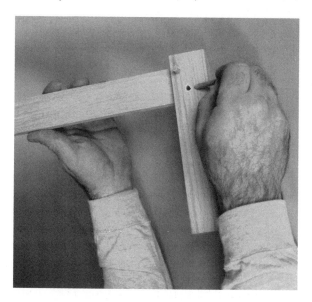

Fig. 18 *Pegs for a pegged mortise-and-tenon joint are inserted into predrilled holes.*

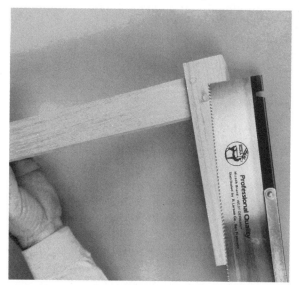

Fig. 19 *After the pegs have been driven in, trim them flush with the wood's face using a backsaw.*

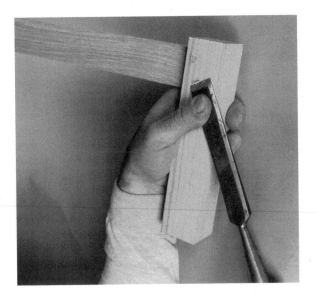

Fig. 20 *After trimming the pegs, clean up the face of the wood with a chisel and sand the pegs smooth and flush.*

Fig. 21 *In a poke-through mortise-and-tenon joint, the tenon protrudes through the wood.*

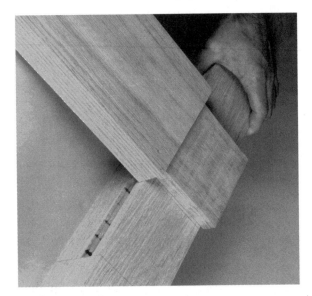

Fig. 22 *To determine how far you want a poke-through tenon to protrude, lay the tenon in place on top of the wood and move it in and out to find the length that you prefer.*

is assembled, simply hold the tenon up in place against the mortised stock (see Fig. 22). Depending on the kind of finished look that you want, poke-through tenons can be chamfered, meaning that their edges are chiseled or sanded down to give a tapered look (see Fig. 23A).

Some Mission furniture had poke-through tenons chamfered with a saw so they had an almost smooth look, yet were decidedly tapered on all four sides. A chop saw set at 15 degrees (or lower if possible) can produce an attractive chamfered tenon. After cutting all four sides of the tenon to form a low-sloping four-sided pyramid (see Fig. 23B), sand it lightly, rounding the edges of the cut to your liking. This is a detailing technique used to finish off the poke-through leg tenons on the Morris chair (see page 116).

The Doweled Joint

Doweling is an age-old way of joining wood, but it requires accuracy. Even a small mistake when positioning one of the dowel holes can make the entire joint look crooked. Carefully follow the steps presented here and take your time when constructing these joints.

A dowel is a short, round piece of wood. It is usually grooved (with spiral or straight grooves) to allow glue to flow along its sides. Dowels are available at hardware stores in a variety of diameter sizes (¼ inch, $5/16$ inch, ⅜ inch, ½ inch) with lengths

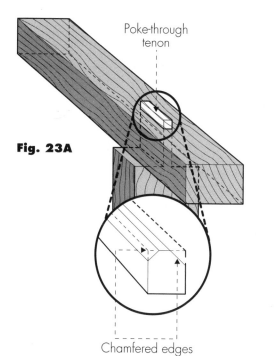

Fig. 23A

Poke-through tenon

Chamfered edges

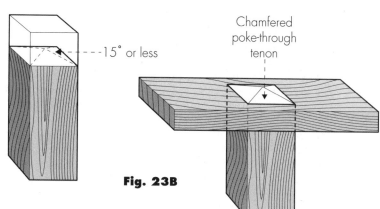

Fig. 23B

15° or less

Chamfered poke-through tenon

Fig. 23A *Chamfer the edges of poke-through tenons to give the joint a more finished look. This can be done with a table saw, or even with a sander.*

Fig. 23B *A classic Mission look employs a poke-through tenon that is cut on four sides at a low angle.*

changing in ¼-inch increments: 1 inch, 1¼ inches, 1½ inches and so on.

When drilling holes for dowels, use a bit the same size as the dowel—a ½-inch drill bit for a ½-inch dowel, a ⅜-inch drill bit for a ⅜-inch dowel and so forth. After you've got your drill loaded with the right bit, positioning the drill holes and keeping your drill square to the face of the board is a real challenge. This task is best done with a doweling jig, a device that is clamped onto the wood so that it lines up and centers a positioning hole that guides your drill bit (see Fig. 24). Most doweling jigs can accommodate a number of different drill bit sizes for a variety of dowel types.

The object of using the doweling jig is to ensure that when adjoining pieces of wood come together, as they will in a joint, the dowel holes match perfectly. Drilling precisely positioned dowel holes with a jig is a two-step process. First, position and clamp the doweling jig on one piece of the wood you want to join, and drill your dowel holes as required by the various projects in this book. After you have one set of dowel holes drilled, there is an easy way to mark the location for the dowel holes on the adjoining wood. (You will use the jig for drilling this second set of holes, but you first need to determine where to clamp the jig.) Simply score the adjoining wood with a pin-point marker, called a "dowel center," and use the mark to guide the position of the doweling clamp and your drill bit.

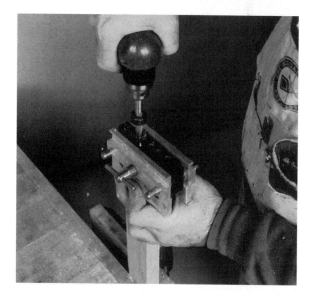

Fig. 24 *A doweling jig is essential for centering and keeping true and square the drill holes into which dowels are inserted.*

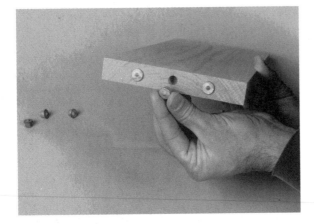

Fig. 25 *Metal dowel centers, temporarily inserted in dowel holes, mark the exact locations for drilling dowel holes in adjoining pieces of wood.*

Fig. 26 *Once dowel centers are inserted, align the adjoining wood, precisely positioned as it will sit in the final joint configuration, and press the board with the dowel centers into it. The dowel center points will leave marks to guide your drill holes.*

After you have the second set of dowel holes drilled, assemble the joint by first squeezing glue into one set of holes. Next, insert the dowels (see Fig. 27). You may have to tap the dowels into the dowel holes with a mallet. With the dowels in place on one piece of wood, apply glue directly from the bottle to the protruding dowels (see Fig. 28), and insert them into the holes of the second piece of wood. Then use a clamp to draw the two pieces of wood together (see Fig. 29). Immediately wipe off any glue that squeezes out from the joint.

Fig. 27 *Once dowel holes are drilled, glue up and insert the dowels. Half of the dowel length should go into the hole, and half should protrude.*

Dowel centers are small, round metal pieces with sharp points protruding from their centers. They temporarily sit inside a dowel hole with the pin-point ends facing out (see Fig. 25). When adjoining wood is pressed against the dowel centers, a mark is left to guide the position of your doweling jig and drill bit. As seen in Fig. 26, sometimes you have to clamp on a ledger to help exactly position the adjoining wood.

Biscuit Joining

It is impossible to find a single hardwood board that is "clear" (knot-free) and wide enough for a tabletop, so to make a large top such as for the dining table (see page 108), you will have to assemble it from narrower boards. The easiest way to join boards for this purpose is with "biscuits." Biscuits are flat, football-shaped slivers of wood, usually made of birch. They range in size from #0 (⅝ inch by 1¾ inches) to #20 (1 inch by 2⅜ inches).

Biscuits work on the same principle as dowels, but because of their shape, they are inserted into

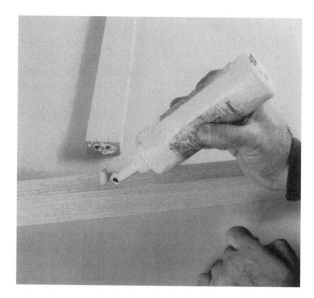

Fig. 28 *Before joining the two pieces of wood with dowels, glue not only the dowels, but also the face of the wood pieces where they will meet.*

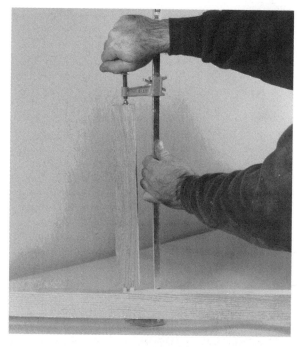

Fig. 29 *Use a clamp to draw the pieces of wood together to make a snug doweled joint.*

flat cuts or "slots" made in the edge or side of a board. The adjoining board is positioned so that its slots match up, and the biscuits join the two pieces, slot to slot.

When biscuits are applied with glue and inserted into the slots, the glue gets absorbed by the biscuits and the biscuits expand. As the glue dries, the biscuits form a very tight joint. The most difficult aspect of biscuit joining is getting the slots to line up exactly.

The slots for a biscuit joint are cut with a tool called a plate joiner or biscuit joiner (see page 30, Fig. 13). After you determine where you want your slots cut on the corresponding boards, you line up the biscuit joiner and plunge the blade into the wood, cutting a slot to the appropriate depth.

Here's a closer look at the process, step by step. First, position your boards as they will sit when they are finally joined. Then, using a square, mark a line on both boards wherever a biscuit will go (see Fig. 30). This line will center the biscuit joiner, so the slots match up. You want at least two biscuits for boards of any length. Space them about 12 inches apart.

The second step is to cut the slots with your

Fig. 30 *When joining boards with biscuits, first position the pieces as they will sit in their final configuration. Then mark a center line for each biscuit.*

biscuit joiner. Use the centering lines you just drew to position your biscuit joiner, and plunge the blade into one board and then into the adjoining board (see Fig. 31).

Fig. 31 *With the center lines as your guide, plunge the biscuit joiner into the board to make the relief cuts for the biscuits.*

Fig. 32 *Glue the edges of the adjoining boards, insert the glue-soaked biscuits and draw the boards together with clamps. Wipe away excess glue, and leave the clamps on until the glue dries.*

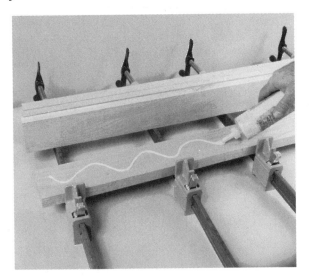

Fig. 33 *When making posts out of pieces of smaller dimension stock, glue the faces of the wood when they are positioned on the clamps.*

Once these slots are cut, apply glue liberally to the biscuits and along the edge of the board. Insert the biscuits in the slots, and use bar or pipe clamps to draw the two boards together and hold them tight (see Fig. 32). Wipe off any glue that squeezes out before it has a chance to dry.

Gluing Up

Since it also is difficult to find full-sized square hardwood boards like the posts used in the Mission couch, you will probably have to create large pieces by gluing together smaller ones. This is easy to do with clamps, glue and a square, but the crucial factor in gluing up stock is getting the final product to the proper dimensions. Ideally, you want to glue up large stock lumber and have the composite piece be exactly the dimension that you need. For instance, the four posts for the Mission couch presented in this book are supposed to be 3¼ inches by 3¼ inches, but you'll have a hard time (or pay a premium custom milling charge) to a get a single board that size. However, it is easy to get actual dimension boards that are ⅞ inch by 3¼ inches. If you glue up four of these, you will have a "post" that is 3¼ inches by 3½ inches. You can choose either to live with the extra ¼ inch or, if you are a purist, to cut that post down to 3¼ inches by 3¼ inches by

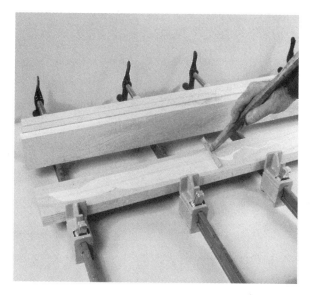

Fig. 34 *After you have applied the glue, smooth it out with a flat stick.*

Fig. 35 *Attach clamps to the top and bottom of the post to ensure a tight bond on both sides.*

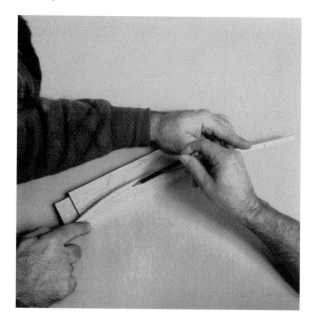

Fig. 36 *To mark a curved cut, a flexible strip of wood can be used to create a gentle arc.*

running it through your table saw. The object of gluing up stock is to get as close as you can to the final dimensions required and to cut off as little as possible.

Gluing up wood is fun and easy. After you have your component pieces chosen, line them up on top of a few bar or pipe clamps and apply glue lib-erally to the boards' faces (see Fig. 33). Then evenly spread the glue around with a flat stick (see Fig. 34). Use a square to position the boards so they are perfectly square at their ends, and clamp the pieces together from both above and below (see Fig. 35).

Making Curved Cuts

Occasionally, you will want to make a curved cut in a piece of stock. Both the bookcase and the coffee table projects (see pages 87 and 94, respectively) call for this. The actual cut can be made with a jigsaw, saber saw or band saw, but first you have to mark the cut line. How is this done? One way is to use a compass: Set the radius you desire and scribe the line. Another method is to take a thin piece of scrap linoleum or a flexible strip of wood and press against the ends to make an arc. Position this on the wood where you want the curved line to be and trace around it with a pencil (see Fig. 36). Or use the bottom of a waste basket, large can or any other appropriately shaped item and trace around it. Then carefully cut along the line you've drawn (see Fig. 37).

Fig. 37 *Cut the curve with a band saw (shown here) or a jigsaw.*

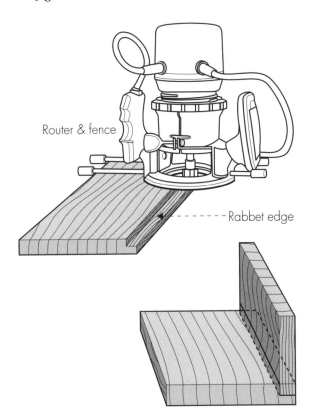

Router & fence

Rabbet edge

Fig. 38 *Use a router and a fence to cut a rabbet joint. Once the rabbet edge is made, the adjoining piece of wood should fit entirely onto the notched-out aspect of the joint.*

Rabbet Joints

The bookcase is the one project that uses a rabbet joint. Rabbet joints are best cut with a router, or with repeated passes with a table saw. You essentially notch out a square edge along the length of a board and fit another board into that notch (see Fig. 38). Although this router technique for joinery is used only once, you also will need a rabbet edge on the inside edges of the hall mirror stiles and rails to create a recess into which you can mount the mirror and its backerboard (see page 56).

Countersinking & Plugging

Two projects in this book require "plugged" countersunk screws: the center post of the dining table (see page 108) and the Morris chair (see page 116). There are other instances where you'll use screws (in the Morris chair seat and when you attach slats to the couch cleats), but these screws will be out of sight and don't need to be hidden with plugs. Plugs are only called for to hide a screw head. A plug is simply a tapered piece of wood that gets glued into a hole that has been recessed so the screw head sits below the surface of the wood (see page 28, Fig. 6).

CHAPTER 3

Finishing & Upholstering

Before you begin to put any finish on your Mission furniture, it has to be properly sanded. So refer back to Chapter 1, "Getting Ready" (see pages 23-25), for a refresher on various sanding tools and techniques.

Next, be sure to remove all the sawdust. Start with the elephant-nose attachment on a shop vac and suck up as much sawdust as possible. Then, wipe down the furniture with a tack cloth, which is cotton cheesecloth that has been dipped in polyurethane. The polyurethane is partially dry, and the cloth is very sticky as a result. It will pick up the last bits of dust. Use a fresh tack cloth for each piece of furniture and replace it if it gets overloaded with sawdust.

Finishes for Mission Furniture

Fuming

In 1909, Gustav Stickley, the master builder of Mission furniture, wrote, "The fact that ammonia fumes will darken new oak was discovered by accident. Some oak boards stored in a stable in England were found after a time to have taken on a beautiful mellow brown tone and on investigation this change in color was discovered to be due to the ammonia fumes that naturally are present in stables.

"The reason for this effect was at first unknown and, to the best of our belief, it was not discovered until the experiments with fuming made in The Craftsman Workshops established the fact that the darkening of the wood was due to the chemical affinity existing between ammonia and tannic acid, of which there is a large percentage present in white oak."

The process of treating white oak to get a "beautiful mellow brown tone" with ammonia fumes is called "fuming." It is what Stickley did and, as he claimed, this fuming process does leave a gorgeous finish on white oak. It is this rich brown hue that we associate with the Mission look.

But why did Stickley treat the oak at all? Why didn't he leave it blond and simply cover it with a varnish? It was Gustav Stickley's intention to give the oak "the appearance which ordinarily would result from age and use." And that's what fuming achieves.

"Oak should be ripened as the old mahogany was ripened by oil and sunshine," Stickley wrote in his book *Craftsman Homes*. "And this can be done only by a process that, without altering or disguising the nature of the wood, gives it the appearance of having been mellowed by age and use. This process is merely fuming with ammonia...."

The fuming process that Stickley used was

rather simple, and—with some care and planning—you can do it too. Since white oak naturally contains tannin, all you have to do to get the desired color is allow ammonia fumes to engulf your piece of furniture in an enclosed space (and watch the coloration process closely!). Stickley experimented with how long to leave the wood exposed to the ammonia, and eventually got fuming down to a science. But since you will likely be doing this for the first time, and for only one or two pieces of furniture, you'll have to start from scratch and use trial and error to determine how long to leave the oak exposed to the ammonia fumes.

There are two main variables that affect the fuming process, and you will have to control them to get the desired finish. First is the moisture content of the wood. If the oak is too dry, the fuming process will not work well, because the ammonia will not be absorbed into the wood. To solve this, Stickley would wet the piece of furniture and let it sit for a few hours to allow the wood pores to open up. Only then would he introduce the ammonia. If your oak is dry, you should do this too. Using a clean nylon paintbrush, liberally apply water as though you were painting the furniture with regular latex paint.

A second variable to watch out for is low tannin content. If you are using well-seasoned or old oak, it may not contain enough tannin to bring about the desired reaction with ammonia. If this is the case, you'll need to add tannin; in fact, it's recommended if you are *at all* worried about low tannic acid content. To make up a tannic acid solution, measure out 3 tablespoons of tannic acid crystals for every 1 cup of warm, distilled water. Liberally apply the solution to the furniture with a clean nylon paintbrush, and let it sit for 24 hours to ensure the solution is absorbed. Only then do you introduce the furniture to the fuming process. (If you can't find tannic acid crystals, boil two dozen acorns for 30 minutes in distilled water and—after the solution cools—apply it to the oak.)

Making Test Scraps. Timing the fuming process takes some experimentation. Before you fume your finished piece of furniture, it is wise to experiment with scraps of wood taken from the same source you used to build your furniture. Observing how these scraps react to ammonia over time will help prevent underfuming (which results in wood that is too light) or overfuming (which makes the resulting finish too dark). After building your airtight compartment (explained below), put in 10 scrap pieces of the wood. Remove one piece every hour, marking it "1 hour," "2 hours," "3 hours" and so on, to give an index of degrees of darkness relative to the duration of exposure to ammonia. From these test pieces, select the desired darkness. Then fume your furniture for the length of time determined by the selected test piece.

The Fuming Compartment. To fume a piece of furniture made of white oak, first complete the construction process and sand the wood with the proper sequence of sandpapers. Postpone attaching any brass or metal fittings for now, as they would be tarnished by the fuming process.

Ammonia Is Poison!

Unfortunately, fuming requires that you work with poisonous industrial-grade ammonia. So take precautions. Wear a long-sleeved shirt and long pants, tight-fitting eye goggles, a carbon-activated-filter mask and industrial-grade rubber gloves. If you get any ammonia on you, wash it off immediately, and follow the exposure procedures written on the ammonia container. Save unused ammonia, if you can, by pouring it back in its container. To dispose of ammonia, wash it down the drain with lots of water. *Don't breathe the fumes under any circumstances.*

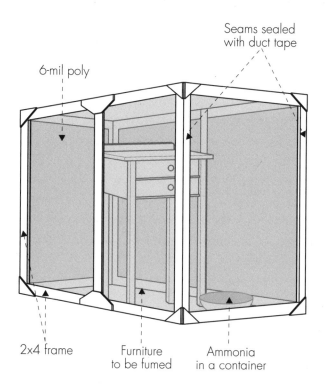

6-mil poly

Seams sealed
with duct tape

2x4 frame

Furniture
to be fumed

Ammonia
in a container

Window

Clean
garbage pail
with
tight-fitting lid

Furniture
to be fumed

Container of ammonia

Fig. 1 *A 2x4 frame covered on all sides, top and bottom with 6-mil polyethylene makes an excellent fuming compartment for large projects.*

Fig. 2 *A clean plastic garbage pail with a tight-fitting lid will accommodate small pieces like the wastepaper basket.*

Next, construct or obtain an airtight compartment of some kind. Depending on the size of the furniture you want to fume, the compartment can be anything from a clean rubber or plastic 30-gallon garbage pail with a secure lid to a 2x4 frame covered with plastic. The compartment must be large enough to hold the piece of furniture and a container of ammonia.

If you choose to build a large compartment, construct it outside, where fresh air will carry away the excess ammonia fumes. (If you *must* be indoors, ensure proper ventilation with fans and open windows.) Construct a simple 2x4 frame, and staple 6-mil polyethylene (clear plastic painter's drop cloth) on all sides, the top and the bottom (see Fig. 1). Overlap the plastic at the seams by 6 inches, and cover the seams with duct tape to ensure a good seal. Use clear rather than black plastic so you

can look in at your piece of furniture to see how dark it is getting with passing time. If you can find only black plastic, create a window of clear plastic so you can check on how your furniture is darkening. If you are fuming in a plastic or rubber garbage pail, cut a window in the lid, cover the opening with clear plastic and secure the plastic with duct tape (see Fig. 2).

Since sunlight beaming in on your furniture during the fuming will affect the color, you may want to cover your fuming compartment with a tarp or blanket to keep out the light.

Fuming with Industrial-Grade Ammonia. Introduce the ammonia to your fuming compartment by pouring it into a quart-size glass or ceramic bowl and placing it inside the compartment. The ammonia you use should be industrial grade, which is

26% ammonia. (Household ammonia—1% to 2% ammonia—will work, but it takes far longer to get the furniture to darken.) Also known as blue-printer's ammonia, industrial-grade ammonia can be obtained from a blueprint firm or a company that makes microfilm copies. If they can't sell you a gallon (it will run about $6), they'll know of a source that can. This is hazardous stuff: note the warnings on page 48.

Once you have your compartment set up and you've run your test strips to determine the approximate desired length of exposure, place your sanded furniture in the compartment with the ammonia and use duct tape to seal up the plastic. Depending on the temperature and humidity, the fuming process with 26% ammonia may take anywhere from 3 to 10 hours or longer. (Some people choose to leave their furniture in the fuming compartment for 48 hours!)

When the furniture finish is darkened to your liking, open the compartment to let the fumes disperse, and remove the furniture. Discard the ammonia by diluting it with plenty of water as you pour it down the sink drain.

You may want to "touch sand" your furniture after it has been fumed. Stickley had his craftsmen lightly sand the wood after fuming "until all the loose fiber is rubbed away and every trace of roughness [is] removed." If you wish, you can do a very light sanding with 220-grit paper, but keep in mind that all the *major* sanding should have been completed before fuming. Touch sanding is done only to remove wood grain that has been raised in the fuming process, which should be minimal. Take care not to sand too heavily, as you risk ruining the finish you've taken such great pains to produce. As a final step, use a tack cloth to remove any resulting sawdust.

Stains

Although fuming is the authentic finish for Mission furniture, it is also the most involved process. A less time-consuming option is to finish your furniture with off-the-shelf stains. The best stains to use are called pigmented stains, and a dependable manufacturer is Minwax.

Granted, you won't obtain the authentic Mission look with these stains (the different aspects of the grain react differently to the stain, giving you a color variation across the board), but you can come close. The finish that most closely approximates fuming can be obtained by a two-step process. First, apply a coat of cherry stain. After it has dried for six hours, take a clean cotton rag and wipe off any lingering wet stain that remains. Allow the piece to sit an additional 18 hours (for a total of 24) and then apply a half-and-half mix of cherry and walnut stains.

To apply the stains, use a cotton rag or a china bristle brush (also called a natural bristle brush). Don't use nylon brushes, as they are designed for water-based coatings and will leave brush marks. You will find that a bristle brush works better than a rag for applying stains because it can more easily reach into nooks and corners. After six hours, wipe away with a clean cotton rag any stain that hasn't been absorbed.

Polyurethane

If you are taking the easy way out and have decided to finish your Mission furniture with off-the-shelf stains, it's a good idea to apply two or three coats of polyurethane on top of the stain for protection once the stain has dried thoroughly. The gloss or satin finish of polyurethane is not true to the original Mission look, but polyurethane's ability to waterproof the wood may be a necessity if you plan to use your furniture in any way or location where it will come in contact with water (off the bottom of drinking glasses or water that overflows when plants are watered, for instance). Applying polyurethane is comparable to coating your furniture with a thin layer of durable plastic.

Polyurethane offers good protection against water and mildew. And if you are going to leave your piece of furniture out in the sun, polyurethane with an ultraviolet blocker (UV blocker) can offer limited protection against the damaging rays of the sun. For outdoor applications, be sure to choose the type of polyurethane carefully, and make sure the label states that the polyurethane blocks ultraviolet light. The label should say something like "exterior-grade" or "UV resistant," or it might have an icon or sketch that shows sunlight being blocked.

There are different finishes in polyurethane, from "satin" to "high gloss." The finish you choose is mostly a matter of looks, because all finish types offer similar protection. The paint store should have some sample blocks that have been painted with the different finishes, so you can compare them with one another.

Since you are going to be using so little polyurethane (probably a gallon *at most*), buy the best you can get your hands on. The work you save by applying a long-lasting, high-quality product will quickly reimburse you for the extra $5 you invested in a premium gallon.

Just before you apply the urethane, vacuum the piece of furniture to remove any sawdust, then wipe it down with a tack cloth. When you get ready to apply the urethane, don't shake the can. Doing so creates bubbles that won't easily settle out. Instead, stir the urethane gently with a paint stick.

Let the first urethane coat dry thoroughly, then lightly sand it with 220-grit sandpaper. This will take down any burrs or grain that the first coat has created. Before applying another coat on top of a sanded coat, use a vacuum and a tack cloth again to pick up any dust.

Paste Filler

If you want an extremely smooth finish (glasslike, with multiple coats) or if you want to dramatically enhance the grain pattern of your wood, use paste filler instead of stain. After the paste filler has been properly applied (described below), you can

use polyurethane or shellac and wax on your furniture for the final coats of protection just as you would treat a piece that has been traditionally stained.

Paste filler is a blend of silex (crushed quartz) and pigments in a suitable vehicle that contains driers and binders. (It costs about $13 a quart.) It can be thinned with naphtha or mineral spirits, and should be applied with a natural bristle brush (not sprayed). Once it has dried within the pores of the wood, the wood cannot be stained—the paste filler blocks absorption of the stain.

Paste fillers are available in a range of stock colors, but can be custom mixed with Japan colors to produce any color filler. (Japan colors are pure pigments that can be used to color oil-based—never water-based—varnish, stains and fillers.) If you mix up a custom color, be sure to make enough for your entire piece of furniture, because it is hard to match the color exactly on subsequent mixes.

To accentuate the grain, apply a paste filler that contrasts with the wood's natural color. For white oak, you'd want to use a darker filler. The darker filler will be absorbed into the pores (the open-grain wood) and give you dramatic grain highlights. For Mission furniture, the best tint color to use is black. Using a quart of paste filler, mix in a tablespoon or two of black Japan color. Add turpentine and mix until the paste filler has the same consistency as heavy cream.

To apply paste filler, get a good stiff, bristle brush. Work against the grain, forcing the paste filler up into the pores. As the paste filler starts to set up, take a rag (a clean cotton towel is ideal; a smooth poly-blend cloth is the worst choice) and stroke against the grain to remove excess paste filler. As you are wiping the wood clean, you may notice places where the paste filler hasn't been absorbed by the open-grain wood. Work it into the pores with your cloth if you have to. You want the paste filler to be in the wood's pores, not just on the surface of the wood. If you find that you started the wipe-down too late and some of the paste filler has dried on the wood, use turpentine or mineral spirits to remove it. When you are done, allow the paste filler to harden for 24 hours. Then lightly sand with the grain with 220-grit sandpaper. After sanding, wipe with a tack cloth to pick up any resulting sawdust.

Shellac

One of the three most popular finishes used by the original makers of Mission furniture was shellac. Shellac is a type of varnish consisting of lac carried in alcohol as a solvent. The word "shellac" has two possible origins, both of which explain what shellac is. Some think the word is a combination of the words "shell" and "lac," as one applies a protective coat or shell using lac dissolved in alcohol. A more probable explanation is that the *Carteria lacca*, or lac tree, produces a resin-encrusted twig called "stick-lac." The resin is cracked off the tree's twigs and dissolved in water to separate it from its reddish color. This is called "seed-lac." The seed-lac is formed into thin plates called "shell-lac," which are broken apart to produce shellac flakes of refined lac. It is these flakes, when mixed with denatured alcohol, that give us true shellac.

Many original Mission furniture makers would first fume the furniture, then shellac it, applying two coats. On top of the shellac, they would apply two coats of wax. As one writer put it in a 1909 book *Mission Furniture: How to Make It*, the wax-and-shellac finish could be "renewed at any time by wiping with a little turpentine and rewaxing."

Stickley himself recommended that after fuming, the furniture be lightly sanded and treated with two coats of thin lacquer, made of one-third white shellac and two-thirds denatured alcohol. (In 1912, denatured alcohol was called "German lacquer.") Note that Stickley called for "thin shellac."

The shellac available at your local hardware store is called "three-pound cut" shellac, meaning that 3 pounds of shellac flakes were dissolved into 1 gallon of denatured alcohol. Unfortunately, this is too thick for obtaining the authentic Mission look (it dries with a high gloss). Three-pound-cut shellac needs to be thinned, despite the claims you may read elsewhere that 3-pound cut is "recommended for furniture." For Stickley, the ideal mixture was 1 pound of shellac to 1 gallon of denatured alcohol.

One easy way to obtain thin shellac is to mix it yourself. You can buy shellac flakes for about $13 a pound through any good woodworking supply house or catalog. Orange shellac is the standard grade and it's what this book recommends, but you can purchase "super blonde" shellac at the high end or "seed-lac" at the low end. Shellac flakes should be dissolved in Behkol, which sells for about $16 a gallon. The directions on the shellac box will give you mixing instructions, but the general formula is to mix 4 ounces of shellac flakes into 1 quart of Behkol.

If you don't want to mix your own shellac, buy a gallon of off-the-shelf 3-pound cut shellac and "cut" it with 2 quarts of denatured alcohol.

In both cases mentioned here (mixing shellac yourself or buying it and cutting it), you should strain the shellac through three layers of cheesecloth to remove chunks, grit and other foreign material. Also, date the final container, because shellac has a six-month shelf life. It dries out and becomes unusable after that.

Apply shellac with a natural bristle brush and stroke it out so the coverage is smooth and evenly distributed. Let it dry overnight. Between coats, sand with 220-grit sandpaper. After sanding, rub down the furniture with a tack cloth.

Wax

After shellac has been applied, it's time to wax the furniture. You should apply two coats of wax. The best wax to use is carnauba wax (not beeswax). Carnauba is available from any good woodworking supply house or catalog. It comes in three colors: clear, orange and dark, and costs about $10 a pound. Use clear to apply to your shellacked surface. Often the wax is hard to apply because it is so thick, so you may have to thin it with turpentine. Once the wax is applied, it will start to set up in about 15 minutes. After it's set, you can buff it to a high gloss. To save on elbow grease, use an auto buffing pad attached to the chuck of your drill.

Before applying a second coat, let the wax dry for the amount of time recommended by the manufacturer, usually 24 hours.

Tung Oil

Not every Mission furniture builder wants an authentic dark Mission finish to his or her furniture. Many want to keep the wood blond or unfinished. The coffee table pictured on page 72 shows a blond finish, achieved by merely treating the wood with tung oil.

Tung oil is an excellent water-resistant oil obtained from the seed of aleurite trees that grow in Japan and China. It protects the wood, yet leaves the natural look and color of the wood largely intact. It tends to give wood a golden glow.

To apply tung oil, first vacuum the furniture and wipe it with a tack cloth. Liberally apply the tung oil with a sponge brush (see Fig. 3) and follow with a clean cotton rag to remove the excess (see Fig. 4).

Upholstering Mission Furniture

Two of the projects presented in this book, the Morris chair and the couch (see pages 116 and 124, respectively), call for upholstered seat cushions. Since you took the time to build an authentic piece of furniture, you may want to finish the job with authentic upholstery as well. But that could be a challenge for you to do yourself.

Here's how seats were created in the original Mission furniture: First, an oak frame was constructed that would sit on cleats installed on the inside of the chair or couch frame once the seat was assembled. Then a truss-and-spring assembly was attached to the oak frame and the springs were covered with burlap. On top of the burlap were two kinds of padding: To give the seat a tuft or crown at its center, a small pile of horsehair or moss was placed in the center of the burlap. Next, three or four layers of cotton felt were added. Then, leather

Fig. 3 *If you prefer a light finish, use tung oil, applied liberally with a sponge brush.*

Fig. 4 *After applying tung oil, wipe up the excess with a clean cotton rag.*

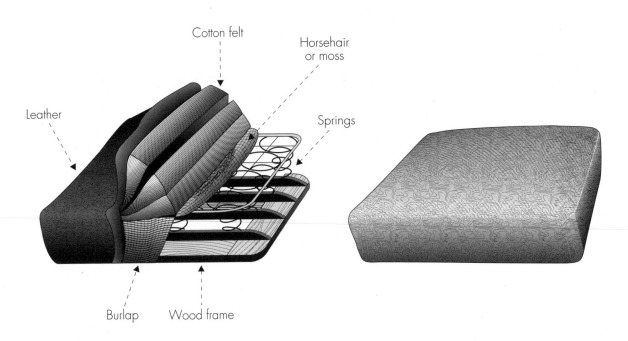

Leather

Cotton felt

Horsehair
or moss

Springs

Burlap   Wood frame

was fitted on top of the cotton and tacked to the underside of the oak frame (see Fig. 5).

Upholstering requires real talent and skill, but even if you are experienced with this kind of work, it may be difficult to find all the right component parts for period-authentic cushions. If you prefer to keep your piece of furniture as true to the period as possible, your best bet is to go to a professional upholsterer and have a seat custom-made.

A less costly option (though not strictly true to the period) is to use foam for the cushions of your seats, covered with a material of your choice. All you need is some plywood, a hot-glue gun, foam, leather or Naugahyde or fabric and a staple gun or ⅜-inch steel tacks (the kind you drive with a hammer, not the kind used in a bulletin board).

The Upholstering Process

For seat cushions, you'll first need a plywood base. Since the couch is built with supporting slats, you can use ½-inch CDX plywood. For the Morris chair seat cushion, however, you should use thicker, ¾-inch CDX plywood, because there is nothing to support the plywood except the cleats around the edge of the seat frame.

When making either piece, use at least 5-inch-

Fig. 5 *The original Mission cushions consisted of a frame, springs, burlap, horsehair or moss, cotton felt and leather. But you can make your cushions out of foam and plywood, covered with a fabric of your choice.*

thick foam for the cushions. You may even want to use 8-inch foam, depending on the density of the foam. Try out the foam by sitting on it in the store. If your weight completely compresses it and you feel the floor when you sit down, then the foam isn't thick enough. Test a few thicknesses until you feel comfortable and the foam supports you.

Cushion foam is available at most fabric and craft shops. If you can't find it there, look up "upholstery" in the Yellow Pages of your phone book and call and ask for a nearby supplier.

Either have the foam cut to the exact size needed or purchase a slightly larger piece and trim it down to size at home, using an electric kitchen knife or a utility or razor knife. The size cushion you use depends on the size of the plywood base. The cushion should *exactly* match the size of the plywood base.

Before purchasing leather, Naugahyde or fabric, measure the dimensions of your base plywood. Let's say the base is 2 feet by 2 feet (or 24 inches

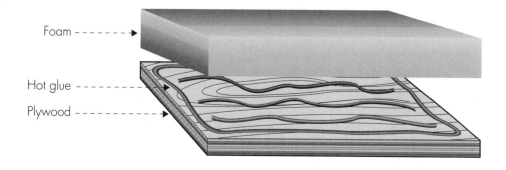

Foam - - - - - - >
Hot glue - - - - - - - -
Plywood - - - - - - - >

Fig. 6 *Attach the foam to the plywood with glue.*

by 24 inches). When gauging how much upholstery material you need, take this 24-inch dimension and add to it the thickness of the foam plus an additional few inches for tacking onto the plywood base. For example, if your cushion is 8 inches high, the length of your material must be 24 inches, plus 8 inches plus 8 inches, plus an ample 4 inches extra on the sides, for a total of 8 more inches. That's 24 + 8 + 8 + 8 = 48 inches, or 4 feet. To upholster a 2-foot by 2-foot seat cushion with 8-inch foam, you'll need a 4-foot by 4-foot piece of material.

Use a hot-glue gun to attach the foam to the base. Apply glue to the plywood (see Fig. 6), and position the foam over it. Next, lay the leather, Naugahyde or fabric *good side down* on a clean work surface, then place the foam-and-plywood assembly on top of it, foam side down (see Fig. 7).

With the material pulled taut against the foam —but not compressing it—work along one side at a time, wrapping the material up over the side and onto the plywood base. Tack (the leather) or staple (the Naugahyde or fabric) in place. Overlap and

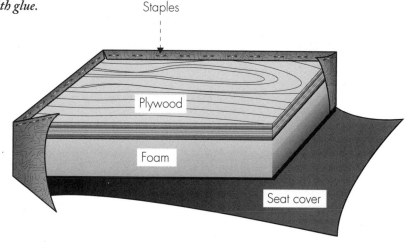

Staples

Plywood

Foam

Seat cover

Fig. 7 *With the "good side" of the cushion material face down, set the foam-and-plywood assembly on top of it, foam side down. Then wrap the material up, around and onto the back side of the plywood, and secure it in place with tacks or staples.*

neatly fold the excess material at the corners and fasten it in place, then continue along the remaining sides, careful all the while to keep the material smooth and taut as you go. When you are done, trim off any excess with a razor knife.

For the back of the Morris chair, you won't need a plywood base for upholstering the cushion. That cushion should be a sewn cushion or pillow that rests in place directly against the stiles and rails.

CHAPTER 4

Hall Mirror

This Mission mirror is a simple woodworking project, great for building skills for the harder furniture projects presented elsewhere in this book. Mortise-and-tenon joints join the wood at the four corners of the mirror, and a router is used to create a channel or recess in which the mirror and its backerboard will sit. Perhaps best of all, this project allows you to get a feel for what it is like to work with a hard wood, without risking very much of an investment in expensive wood stock.

A 1907 magazine article in *The Craftsman*, which Gustav Stickley edited, claimed that "one piece of furniture that is well-nigh indispensable is the hall mirror. The model shown here [has a] severity in design, all its charm depending on the nicety of proportion and workmanship. The corners [are] mortise and tenon construction, with the tenons projecting slightly and very carefully finished." Stickley suggested using brass, iron or copper hat hooks on either side of this mirror, the choice of metal depending on the tone of the finish you put on the wood. The mirror is designed to be suspended by a chain, though you also could mount it on the wall as shown above.

In the original Mission design, the top crosspiece of this mirror had a very slight curve or peak, but to simplify this project, we've made it a straight piece of oak stock.

CUT LIST AND MATERIALS

TOP RAIL: (1) 1⅛x3½-inch oak, 38½ inches long

BOTTOM RAIL: (1) 1⅛x3-inch oak, 38½ inches long

STILES: (2) 1⅛x3½-inch oak, 27 inches long

OAK PEGS: (4) 1¼-inch-long, ¼x¼-inch chamfered oak pegs

MIRROR: (1) 19⅜x31⅜-inch mirror

BACKERBOARD: (1) ¼-inch lauan plywood, 19⅜x31⅜ inches

BRACKETS: (4) 4-inch flat metal brackets

SCREWS: (8) ½-inch flathead wood screws

EYE HOOKS: (2) ½-inch eye hooks

CHAIN: (1) 48-inch-long chain

GLUE: Yellow carpenter's glue

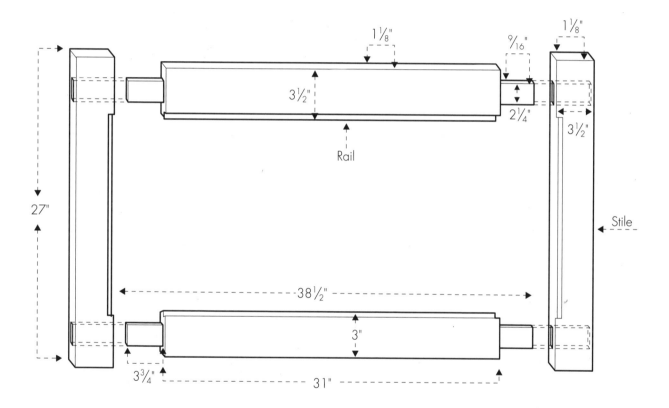

The Rails & Stiles

This Mission mirror consists of two rails (horizontal pieces) and two stiles (vertical pieces). The stiles have mortises cut entirely through them. The rails have true tenons cut into their ends, and they extend through the stiles to become poke-through tenons. The mortise-and-tenon joints are pegged, which adds stability to the mirror, keeps the joints

Fig. 1 *This exploded view of the mirror frame (showing the back side) includes the edge routing that will allow a mirror and backerboard to sit flush with the back of the stiles and rails. Note that the rails are routed along their entire length, but the stiles are not.*

intact and provides a simple yet attractive design element.

Note that the top and bottom rails are two different widths; the top rail is ½ inch wider than the bottom rail. This is for subtle proportioning. Cut the top rail from the 1⅛x3½-inch oak to a length of 38½ inches and the bottom rail from the 1⅛x3-inch oak to a length of 38½ inches.

Since the inside measurement of the mirror is 31 inches across, the shoulder-to-shoulder distance of the rails should also be 31 inches and the tenons 3¾ inches long, allowing ¼ inch to poke through on each end. The instructions from Chapter 2, "Joinery" (see page 33), stated that the tenon would normally be one-half the dimension of the wood. But since the rail boards here are 3 inches and 3½ inches wide, respectively, the tenons can be larger. Make them 2¼ inches instead of only 1½ inches. A wider poke-through tenon gives the joint a more substantial look, plus it's a distinctly Mission touch. Using a table saw or router in the manner described on pages 36-37, cut the tenons for both rails so they measure 9/16 inch thick by 2¼ inches wide by 3¾ inches long (see Fig. 1).

If you want to chamfer the ends of your tenons, now is the time to do it. See pages 40 and 41 for chamfering instructions, or, for tenons this small, just chamfer the tenon ends by eye with your elec-

Fig. 2 *Determine the mortise positions by laying out your rails (with the tenons cut in them) exactly as they will sit in the assembled frame.*

tric palm sander. Load the sander with 80-grit paper, and hold it at an angle to the end of the tenon, sanding down the square edges to your liking.

To make the stiles, cut the two pieces of 1⅛x3½-inch oak to a length of 27 inches. To determine where to cut the mortises, set the rails in place so that their inside edges are 19 inches apart (see Fig. 2). Note that the stiles overhang the rails by about ¾ inch on each end, rather than making a flush edge at the top and bottom of the mirror. Mark the placement of the mortises on the stiles and then cut them out as described on pages 34-36.

Routing the Mirror Channels

Before inserting the rails' tenons into the stiles' mortises, you have to rout out a channel along the inside edge for the mirror and backerboard to sit in. A ⅜-inch-wide channel will do. But how deep should it be? When the mirror is laid in place, it will have a backerboard behind it. (In this project, the backerboard is made from lauan plywood, but it can be any similarly stiff ¼-inch sheet material.) The depth of the channel is the combined thickness of the mirror and the backerboard sandwiched together. Measure their combined thicknesses, then rout out the channel to this depth, going the full length of both rails (see Fig. 3, and Rabbet

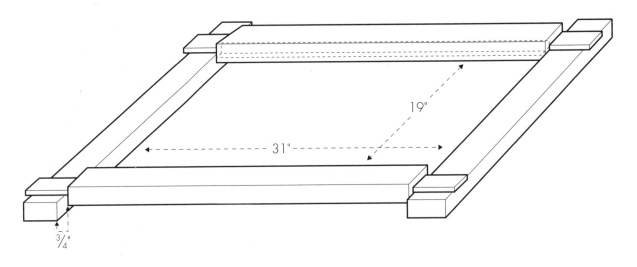

31"

19"

¾"

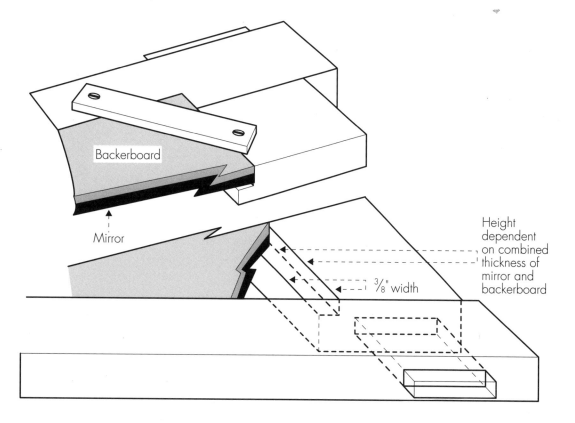

Backerboard

Mirror

Height dependent on combined thickness of mirror and backerboard

³⁄₈" width

Joints, page 46, Fig. 38 for a review of this routing technique).

It will be easier to rout the mirror-and-backerboard channels on the stiles once the rails are in place. Since these channels won't run the entire length of the stiles (as they did on the rails), you need reference points of where to begin and end them. With the rails in place to indicate the length of the channel, rout out a channel on both stiles (see Fig. 4). To hold the stile in place for routing, box it in with wood blocks, screwed into your work table, on both ends and on the side opposite the one you are routing.

Assembling & Pegging the Mirror Frame

Once the channels are routed, glue up and assemble your mirror frame, using the gluing and clamping procedures outlined on page 38. With the mirror frame fit snugly together, it's time to peg the mortise-and-tenon joints, with one peg per

Fig. 3 *When the frame is assembled, the mirror and backerboard will be held in place with flat metal brackets that span the corners.*

corner, centered so each will be driven through the geometric center of the tenon. Using the peg-cutting and drilling procedures discussed on pages 38-39, cut and shape the pegs and drill holes for them. You don't want to drill all the way through the rail or stile stock, so mark your drill bit with a masking tape band so it goes in only ⅞ inch.

Drive the pegs into these holes, then use a backsaw to cut the excess peg flush with the face of the mirror. Clean up any rough edges with a chisel, and use sandpaper to sand down the peg until it is smooth.

Installing the Mirror & Chain

Now it's time to lay the mirror and backerboard in place and properly secure them. This is done with four 4-inch flat metal brackets. Each one

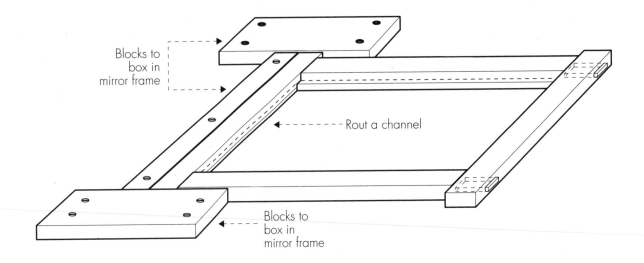

Blocks to box in mirror frame

Rout a channel

Blocks to box in mirror frame

Fig. 4 *Once the mirror frame is assembled, trap it with blocks on a work surface for routing. The blocks will hold the frame in place as you rout out the mirror channels.*

should span a corner, trapping the backerboard and mirror beneath it (see Fig. 3). Screw the brackets in place with the ½-inch flathead wood screws that come in the same package.

If you want to hang the mirror with a chain, as Stickley recommended, attach two sturdy ½-inch eye hooks to the back of the frame. Where you place the eye hooks and how long the chain is (48 inches is recommended) will dictate how much chain you see when the mirror is in place on a wall.

Install the eye hooks one-third of the way down the mirror, on the stiles. Hook up the chain and adjust it, if necessary, until you like what you see.

Finishing the Mission Mirror

When you've completed assembling your Mission mirror, sand off any pencil marks or blemishes that have been left by the assembly process. With poke-through tenons, it's especially important to clean off any dried glue. Use a chisel followed by sandpaper for this task. Then turn to pages 47-53 for instructions on how to fume or finish this piece.

CHAPTER 5

Wastepaper Basket

For the beginning woodworker, this small waste basket is a manageable and satisfying project. It will teach you basic woodworking skills and prepare you for some of the more advanced joinery techniques required in other pieces. In addition, the cost of materials is not particularly high and the end product is both attractive and practical.

This project includes distinctive Mission design features. The corner posts have four-sided pyramidal points and the slats have pointed tops, all of which are easy to cut and nicely accentuate the overall Mission look.

Before starting, keep in mind that the wastepaper basket is rather small: about 19 inches high and 9 inches square. It is well suited for a bathroom or bedroom, or even as a container for a houseplant, but it would probably fill up rather quickly in any modern office.

The Corner Posts

To begin, cut the corner posts. Each post is ¾ inch square and 17 inches long. When you purchase 1-by oak stock, it will have an actual thickness dimension of ¾ inch. But since oak stock is sold in 1x4 or 1x6 dimensions, you will have to cut the ¾x¾-inch post stock from a wider piece of wood. Simply set your table saw at ¾ inch, and run the 1-by stock through the saw lengthwise (called "ripping"). The resulting piece of wood should be ¾ inch by ¾ inch square.

Next, using a chop saw, cut the four posts to a length of 17 inches each. The bottom ends of the posts are square cut, but the tops have four 45-degree-angle cuts that form a peak, like a four-sided pyramid. To make these, use a chop saw (or

CUT LIST AND MATERIALS

CORNER POSTS: (4) ¾x¾x17-inch oak pieces

RAILS: (4) ¾x¾x7½-inch oak pieces

BOTTOM PIECE: (1) 1x9-inch-square oak board

BLOCKS: (4) ¾x¾x1-inch oak blocks

SLATS: (12) ¼x¾-inch oak, 18 inches long

DOWELS: (8) 1¼-inch-long, ¼-inch-diameter wood dowels

DOWEL CENTERS: (2) ¼-inch-diameter metal dowel centers

GLUE: Yellow carpenter's glue

SCREWS:
(4) 2½-inch-long #8 flathead screws
(24) ¾-inch-long #8 roundhead screws

Cutting Tops of Corner Pieces
4 views of one piece

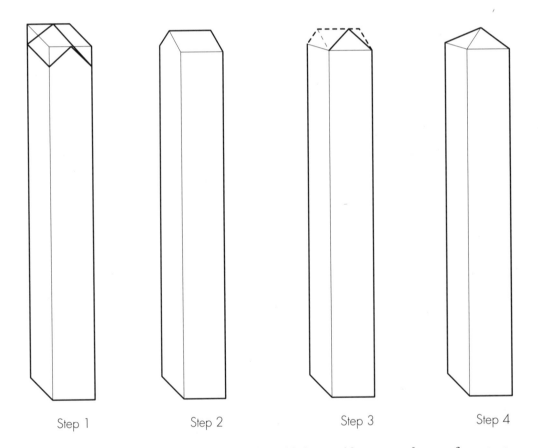

Step 1   Step 2   Step 3   Step 4

Fig. 1 *Use a chop saw to make each of the cuts for a four-sided pyramid crown on the tops of your posts.*

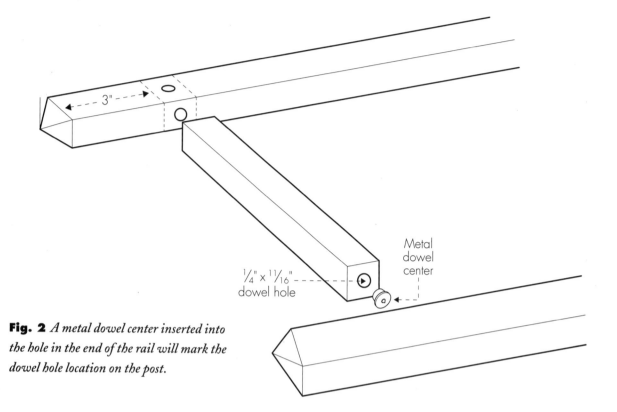

Fig. 2 *A metal dowel center inserted into the hole in the end of the rail will mark the dowel hole location on the post.*

a handsaw in a miter box), and nip the top corners off at 45 degrees on all four sides (see Fig. 1).

The Top Rails

The corner posts are joined together at the top by four 7½-inch-long rails that are doweled into the posts. Cut the rails from the same ¾x¾-inch wood that you used for the corner posts.

Next, drill the holes for the ¼-inch wood dowels in the ends of the four rails. Drill a ¼-inch-diameter hole into the center of both ends of each rail, using a doweling jig to guide your drill bit (see page 41, Fig. 24). Since each dowel is 1¼ inches long, and half of it will be inserted in each dowel hole, the depth of the hole needs to be ⅝ inch, plus ¹⁄₁₆ inch to accommodate excess glue, for a total of 1¹¹⁄₁₆ inches. When you have finished drilling, clean out the dowel holes so they are free of sawdust.

Now you need to locate where to drill the dowel holes in the posts. To do this, insert a metal dowel center into one of the holes drilled in the rails (see Fig. 2). Position the top edge of a rail so that it is 3 inches down from the topmost point of a post and press the pieces together. The dowel center will leave a mark to guide the placement of your doweling jig. Repeat this with the remaining rails and corner posts. You will end up marking eight dowel holes in the posts. Make sure you mark to drill these holes on adjacent faces of the posts.

After you have marked the centers for the dowel holes, carefully clamp your doweling jig onto a post, and drill a ¼-inch-diameter hole 1¹¹⁄₁₆ inches deep. Turn the post to where the other dowel hole should go and repeat this drilling procedure. Do the same for the remaining three posts. You may find that the dowel holes intersect inside your posts. If this happens, you may have to trim four of your dowels, using a backsaw, so they don't butt into the opposing dowels in each post.

Next, glue up the eight 1¼-inch-long wood dowels and insert them into the four rails, using the doweling techniques described on pages 40-42.

(continued on page 73)

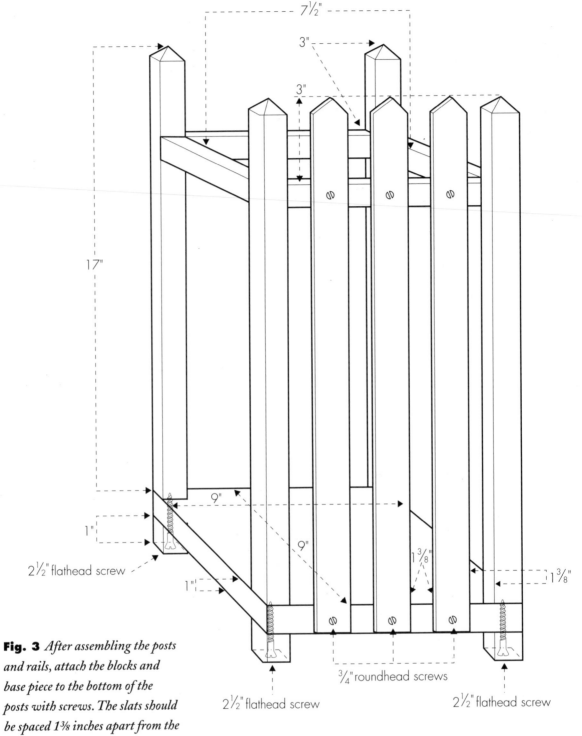

7½"

3"

3"

17"

9"

9"

1"

1³⁄₈"

1³⁄₈"

1"

2½" flathead screw

2½" flathead screw

2½" flathead screw

¾" roundhead screws

Fig. 3 *After assembling the posts and rails, attach the blocks and base piece to the bottom of the posts with screws. The slats should be spaced 1⅜ inches apart from the posts and from each other, and their tops should be at the same height as the top of the posts.*

Magazine Table, page 102 and Wastepaper Basket, page 61

Bed Stand, page 80

Morris Chair, page 116

Dining Table, page 108

Couch or "Box Settle," page 124

Bookcase, page 87

Hall Mirror, page 56 and Tabletop Lamp, page 74

Coffee Table, page 94

Lightly tap them into the dowel holes until they won't go any farther.

Then glue up and insert the rail dowels into the post dowel holes. Use a steel square to make sure all these posts and rails join at 90 degrees. When you have all the dowels inserted and the assemblage aligned for square, clamp it with bar clamps for the time recommended on the container of glue you are using, or for at least one hour.

The Bottom Piece & Blocks

The bottom of the wastebasket is a 1x9-inch-square piece of oak. If you have trouble finding oak of this size, you may have to assemble this from two other pieces and join them together with biscuits, as described on pages 42-44.

The bottom piece will be secured to the posts later with screws, but for now, simply glue it to the underside of the four corner posts, aligning all edges perfectly (see Fig. 3).

Next, you will attach the four blocks to the underside of the bottom piece, one in each corner, using 2½-inch #8 flathead screws. Each block should be ¾x¾-inch square and 1 inch long. Before inserting the screws, predrill a ³⁄₃₂-inch-diameter hole all the way though each block and all the way through the bottom piece, and start a pilot hole in the center of the underside of the post (see page 27 for predrilling instructions). Predrilling the holes helps prevent the wood from splitting. Then align all edges so they are square and flush and insert a screw through the block and the bottom piece and into the corner post (see Fig. 3), screwing until the screw head is slightly recessed in the underside of the block. Repeat this process at the remaining three corners.

The Slats

The 12 slats, three on each side, are made from ¼x¾-inch pieces of oak cut to 18-inch lengths. They are held in place with ¾-inch-long roundhead screws, inserted through the center of the outside face of each slat at the top and bottom. At the top, the screws attach to the rails; at the bottom, the screws go into the bottom piece.

Cut the slats square at the bottom and at opposing 45-degree angles at the top. It is easiest to make the angled cuts with a chop saw. To do this, lay a piece of slat stock in the chop saw, cut a 45-degree angle, then flip the piece over to cut the opposing side of the angled peak.

Since you will be screwing these slats into place, it is essential to predrill pilot holes for the screws in the slats.

Next, lay the slats in place with 1⅜ inches between each one, and with 1⅜ inches between each slat and corner post (see Fig. 3). Screw the slats in place with ¾-inch roundhead screws.

Once you have the entire piece assembled, sand it according to the instructions on pages 23-25.

CHAPTER 6

Tabletop Lamp

This handsome lamp is quintessentially Mission in its lines and form. Here Stickley has definitely abandoned the curved lines and florid patterns of the Victorian age for an austere and simple crossbar design from which hangs two lamps.

Although it appears to be an easy project, this lamp calls for mid-level joinery and router skills, as well as some familiarity with wiring. Consequently, if you are new to woodworking, you may want to try the mirror (see page 56) or wastepaper basket (see page 61) before taking on this project. Here's why: Constructing the post and inserting it into the two base pieces is somewhat difficult. Because the post is almost 2 feet high, the slightest mistake in the base joinery will exaggerate itself by tilting the post. The second challenge is the wiring. Fishing the lamp cord through the post and into the cross bar re-

quires not only patience but also exact bore hole placements. That said, don't be scared off too quickly. With a little determination and careful use of your router, saw and drill, you can produce a fine, authentic Mission piece, while honing your skills for larger, more difficult projects.

The original design for this lamp has the electrical cord coming out of the top of the post. Stickley probably did this for simplicity's sake. If this seems unsightly, you can modify the design so that the cord exits from the back of the post at the crossbar level. Another alternative is to bore out the post and run the lamp cord from its base, or even from the underside of the base pieces.

Once you have the cord holes drilled and the lamp cord fished through the post and cross bar, the actual wiring of the lamp is very basic, and if

CUT LIST AND MATERIALS

POST: (1) 1½x1½-inch oak, 24 inches long

CROSS BAR: (1) ¾x1⅛-inch oak, 14½ inches long

UPPER BASE PIECE: (1) 6x6-inch oak, ¾ inch thick

LOWER BASE PIECE: (1) 9x9-inch oak, 1 inch thick

LAMP CORD: (1) 8-foot length of standard brown lamp cord, trimmed to required length

WIRE NUTS: (2) ¼-inch wire nuts

GLOBES OR SHADES: (2) globes or shades

STEEL PLATE (optional): (4) 2x2-inch steel plates or (1) 6x6-inch steel plate (ask at a machine shop)

LIGHT FIXTURES:
(2) brass caps
(2) socket shells with "uno" thread brackets
(2) on/off sockets
(2) globe hangers
(1) lamp plug

EPOXY: (1) package general-purpose two-part "five minute" tube epoxy

FELT: (1) 12x12-inch felt piece to cut and cover the steel plates

GLUE: Yellow carpenter's glue

you have any experience with wiring lamps or household wiring, you can easily accomplish this job. If you are the least bit uncomfortable about working with the cord connections, take the lamp to a local lamp shop before it is entirely assembled and ask the folks there to wire it up for you. As you will see, you can then tuck the cords up into the underside of the cross bar and proceed with the remaining steps for this project.

The Post

To begin, cut the post from the 1½x1½-inch oak to a length of 24 inches. The post is square cut at its top, but has a true tenon at its bottom. In order for the tenon to protrude through the ¾-inch-thick upper base piece and almost all the way through the 1-inch-thick lower base piece of the lamp, it needs to be 1⅜ inches long. As discussed earlier, a tenon should be at least one-half the stock dimension, so the thickness and height of the tenon should measure ¾ inch by ¾ inch. Cut this on your table saw using the techniques described on pages 36-37.

Next, cut a slot through the post for the cross bar. This slot is essentially a mortise, and it can be cut with either a router using the mortising skills discussed on pages 34-36, or—more easily—with a mortising bit on a drill press.

If you use the mortising bit, the sides of the slot will be straight and square and need only a light touch-up with a chisel. But if you use a router, which has a round bit and can only get so far into the corners, you will have to square the corners of the slot with a sharp chisel.

How big should the slot be and where should it be positioned? Since the cross bar measures ¾ inch by 1⅛ inches, the slot is cut to those same dimensions. The top of the slot should be 1½ inches down from the top of the post and the slot itself should be centered within the body of the post (see Fig. 1).

To accommodate the wires (lamp cord) that will run to the fixtures suspended from the cross bar, you have to drill a small ⅛-inch-diameter hole (or whatever the thickness of your lamp cord) down from the top, dead center of the post and into the slot where the cross bar will go (see Fig. 2).

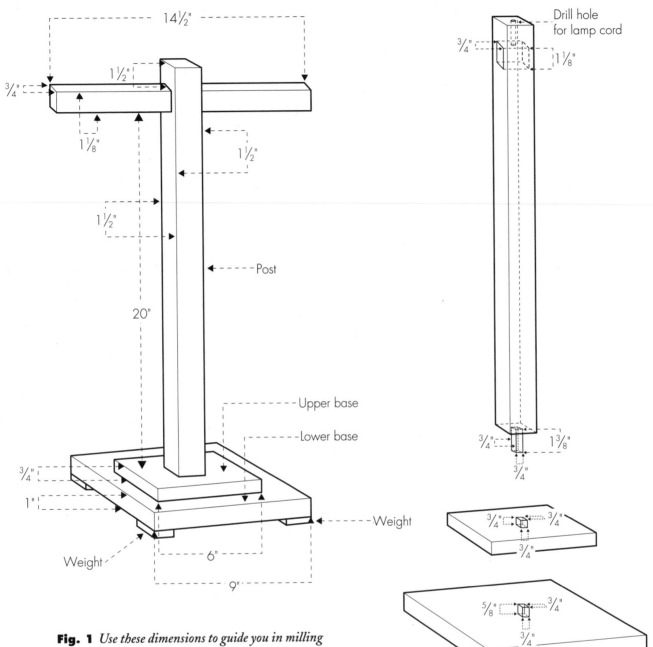

Fig. 1 *Use these dimensions to guide you in milling and assembling the component pieces of the lamp and locating your crossbar mortise.*

Fig. 2 *The ¾-inch-square tenon at the base of the post is a true tenon, milled out of the post wood. It is 1⅜ inches long and fits into the mortises cut in the two base pieces.*

The Base Pieces

There are two base pieces, an upper one and a lower one, of different sizes. The upper base piece is ¾ inch thick and 6 inches square. The lower base piece is 1 inch thick and 9 inches square. You may have to assemble these from smaller pieces of wood, joined with biscuits, using the techniques described on pages 42-44.

Once you have the base pieces cut (and biscuit joined, if necessary) to the proper dimensions, you need to find their dead center. For this you'll use an old carpenter's technique. To find the center of any square, measure diagonally from one corner to the other and mark the midpoint along this line. In a perfect square, this midpoint should be the center, but to double-check this, measure diagonally from the other two corners and mark the midpoint of that line. These two midpoints should be in exactly the same place—the center of the square. Use this technique on both base pieces to find where you will create the mortise for the base of the post.

Now, using a mortising bit on a drill press, or a router, cut out a ¾x¾-inch square mortise all the way through the center of the 6x6-inch base piece. For the lower base piece, cut out a ¾x¾-inch mortise (also centered) that is ⅝ inch deep. Clean up and square the sides with a chisel. When you stack the base pieces on top of each other, the mortises should line up perfectly, with even borders of the lower base piece revealed on all four sides.

Assembling the Pieces

It's best to attach the two base pieces at the same time you insert the post tenon through them. Use the techniques described on page 44 to glue up the two base pieces. While the glue is still wet, glue and insert the post tenon through the mortises you have cut in the centers of the base pieces. This assembly will be difficult to clamp, because of its odd configuration, but you need to clamp it for the en-

tire drying time recommended by the glue manufacturer (usually one hour for yellow carpenter's glue). Place a stiff 9-inch-long board on top of the post, and use it to clamp the assemblage together.

The Cross Bar

Making the cross bar requires several steps. First, cut the cross bar from the ¾x1⅛-inch oak to a length of 14½ inches. Square off each end with a chop saw. Then drill a small (⅛ inch) hole, centered, at the halfway mark along the cross bar's top edge (see Fig. 3). The hole should be the same diameter as your lamp cord. Next, rout up from the center bottom of the cross bar to create a straight slot 4 inches long and ½ inch wide, which is wide enough to contain two wire nuts. When the lamp is wired, the lamp cord coming in from the top of the post will be connected to two other lamp cords: one running to the left and one running to the right, which will bring power to each lamp. The routed slot will accommodate the wire nuts where three cord paths connect.

Next, you need to drill a passageway for the cords that run from the routed slot to where the lamps dangle from the cross bar. This is a two-step process.

First, drill a ⅛-inch hole (or the diameter of your lamp cord) up from the underside of the cross bar exactly above where you want the lamps to dangle. This hole should be drilled only halfway into the crossbar stock. Connect this just-drilled hole with the routed slot by drilling a second hole, this time in a horizontal direction. Since it is difficult to get a drill into this routed slot, you may have to drill this connecting hole at a slight angle, using a long ⅜-inch bit, or even a spade bit, which gives you extra length. The object here is to create a passage from the routed slot to the hole above where the lamps will dangle (see Fig. 3).

To assemble the post and cross bar, fish the lamp cord down through the hole you drilled in the

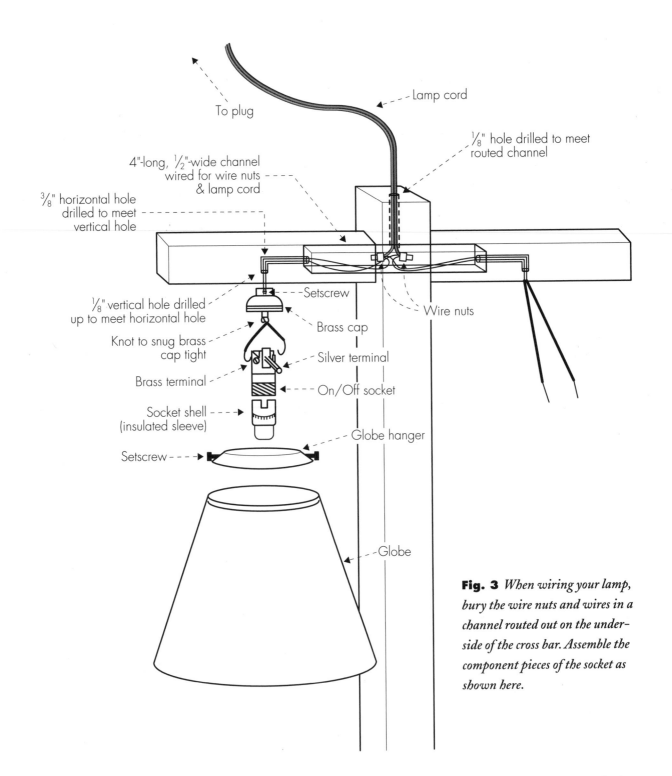

To plug

Lamp cord

$\frac{1}{8}$" hole drilled to meet routed channel

4"-long, $\frac{1}{2}$"-wide channel wired for wire nuts & lamp cord

$\frac{3}{8}$" horizontal hole drilled to meet vertical hole

Setscrew

$\frac{1}{8}$" vertical hole drilled up to meet horizontal hole

Wire nuts

Brass cap

Knot to snug brass cap tight

Silver terminal

Brass terminal

On/Off socket

Socket shell (insulated sleeve)

Globe hanger

Setscrew

Globe

Fig. 3 *When wiring your lamp, bury the wire nuts and wires in a channel routed out on the underside of the cross bar. Assemble the component pieces of the socket as shown here.*

top of the post, and maneuver the cross bar so you can fish this cord out of the routed slot. Pass two other pieces of lamp cord (one on each end of the cross bar) up through the holes you drilled on the underside of the cross bar. Join the wires with wire nuts (see Fig. 3), and push the wire nuts and wire up and out of sight into the routed slot. You may even want to epoxy these wires in place to keep them from hanging down or bulging out beyond the confines of the slot.

After all the wires are in place, you can glue the cross bar in place. There will be some play in the cross bar, as you'll notice when sliding it back and forth to run and adjust the wires. To glue it, slide the cross bar out of position and use a small brush to apply glue to the part that will be hidden by the post once it's back in place. Then carefully slide the cross bar back into position. The amount of glue used will be minimal, as a little bit will go a long way to stabilizing this already tight joint.

Wiring the Sockets

Using the materials listed on page 75 and referring to Fig. 3, assemble the sockets and globe hangers. The sockets will come with a wiring diagram, but most sockets work the same way, with two contact screws on each socket, one for each of the two leads on the lamp cord. The topmost part of the socket will have a brass cap with a setscrew that cinches down on the lamp cord. Slide this brass cap up tight to the underside of the cross bar, and set the screw. When the on/off socket is attached to this cap, it will keep the fixture from sliding down the lamp cord under the weight of the globe.

Separate the two lamp cord strands and tie a simple knot in both, but before pulling it tight, slide the knot up to the underside of the brass cap and then cinch it tight. This will further protect the fixture from sliding.

Next, strip back ½ inch of the cord insulation from each of the two wire cord leads, and wrap the copper strands clockwise around the contact screws. Tighten the screws down on the wires and slide the socket's insulating cardboard sleeve into place, carefully following the directions that came with the socket shells. Finally, attach the globe hangers to the socket shells. Each globe hanger will have setscrews that tighten down on the globes to hold them in place.

All these fixtures are available at most electrical supply houses, and configurations may differ, depending on the kind of socket and globe or shade you purchase. You might want to bring an illustration of the lamp to the store and ask the clerk to assemble the fixtures for you. Green banker's shades look great with this lamp, but you can choose the ones you want from an illustrated catalog at the electrical supply house.

Weighting the Base

The lamp can stand on its own very well, but to give it even more stability, you may want to attach small squares of steel in each corner of the bottom base piece, or just attach a steel plate to the underside of the bottom base piece. With a little epoxy and some felt, you can pad the steel weights or plate to keep them from scratching any furniture the lamp rests on.

Once you have the entire piece assembled, sand it according to the instructions outlined on pages 23-25, then finish it as desired (see pages 47-53).

CHAPTER 7

Bed Stand

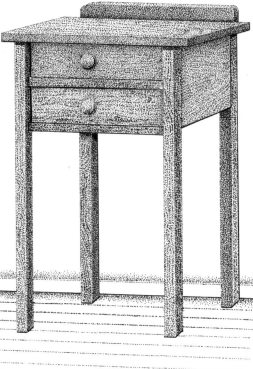

The Craftsman magazine described this table as being "primarily designed for use in a bedroom, to stand near the bed and hold a lamp, candle or one or two books, but it is convenient in any place where a small stand is needed."

This practical table could be placed in a hallway or made in duplicate pairs and set on either side of a couch or, as The Craftsman suggested, on either side of a bed.

As for carpentry skills, the only challenging aspect of building this table is making the drawers. Stickley called for them to be dovetailed, but dovetailing is a difficult wood-joining technique. If you know how to dovetail (or even use finger joints), you can follow Stickley's original prescription. If not, simplify the drawers by butt-joining them together with dowels, as we have suggested below in the instructions and the drawings. The rest of the table can be easily assembled, with the joinery accomplished with a router, drill and table saw.

The Tabletop

As with other projects in this book that call for large 1-inch-thick pieces of oak, you will have to make the tabletop from two or more narrower boards that are joined together with biscuits. Referring to the directions on pages 42-44, cut and assemble the oak boards for the tabletop so that it measures 21 inches across and 17½ inches deep. Glue, join and clamp the boards, and let the tabletop sit for at least one hour to allow the glue to set up.

To make the riser that sits on the back end of the tabletop, cut a 1x1½-inch oak board to a length of 18 inches. Round off the riser's top corners by marking the curves with a compass or tracing along the edge of a can, and cutting them with a jigsaw (see page 45).

Next, mark a line 1 inch in from the back edge of the tabletop, running parallel to the 21-inch

CUT LIST AND MATERIALS

TABLETOP: (1) 1x17½x21-inch oak

TABLETOP RISER: (1) 1x1½-inch oak, 18 inches long

LEGS: (4) 1½x1½-inch oak, 29 inches long

RAILS:

(2) 1x2¼-inch oak, 16½ inches long, for back rails

(4) 1x2¼-inch oak, 14¼ inches long, for side rails

(2) 1x2¼-inch oak, 16 inches long, for front rails

SIDE PANELS: (2) 1-inch-thick oak, 8x17 inches

BACK PANEL: (1) 1-inch-thick oak, 8x16 inches

DUST PANELS: (2) ⅜-inch birch plywood, 13¼x13¾ inches

DRAWER FRONTS AND BACKS: (4) 1-inch-thick oak, 3¼x15½ inches

DRAWER SIDES: (4) 1-inch-thick oak, 3¼x15 inches

DRAWER BOTTOMS: (2) ⅜-inch birch plywood, 14¾x15¾ inches

KNOB: (2) pull knobs for the drawer fronts

DOWELS: (51) 1-inch-long, ½-inch-diameter wood dowels

DOWEL CENTERS: (4) ½-inch-diameter metal dowel centers

GLUE: Yellow carpenter's glue

Fig. 1 *A 1½-inch-tall riser, with its top corners rounded off, is doweled to the tabletop using ½-inch-diameter dowels.*

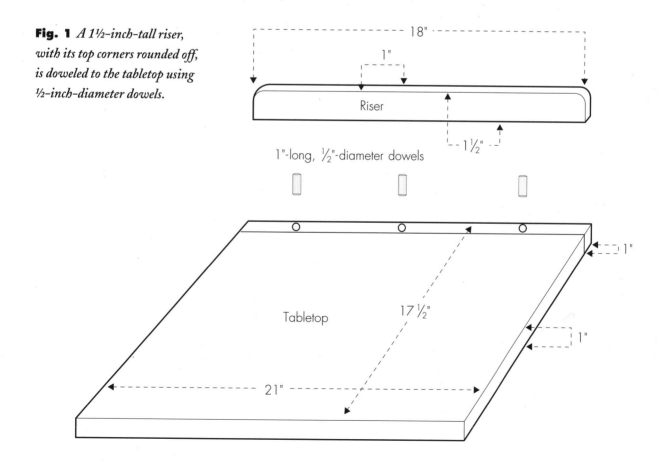

length (see Fig. 1). Centered within this 1-inch-wide band and at least 2 inches in from both sides of the tabletop, drill three evenly spaced ½-inch-diameter holes for the 1-inch-long wood dowels. Each hole should be half the dowel length, plus ¹⁄₁₆ inch to account for excess glue. So that's ½ inch plus ¹⁄₁₆ inch, or ⁹⁄₁₆ inch deep.

Insert metal dowel centers in these holes, position the riser as it will sit when finally joined to the tabletop and apply light downward pressure on the riser so the dowel centers make their marks. Then drill ½-inch-diameter holes ⁹⁄₁₆ inch deep on the underside of the riser. Apply glue to three of the dowels, insert them in the holes in the riser and join it to the tabletop by clamping down on the two pieces of wood with Jorgensen clamps (see page 26, Fig. 5E).

The Legs

Cut each of the legs from 1½-inch-square oak to a length of 29 inches. To get 1½-inch-square oak, start with 2x2 stock, which has an actual dimension close to what you require. Mill it to 1½ inches square by running the stock lengthwise through your table saw.

The legs are joined to the panels with dowels, two for each end of each panel (see Fig. 2). To determine where to drill holes in the legs for these dowels, measure down 8 inches (the height of each panel) from the top of each leg. Make light pencil marks on the legs to indicate where the side and back panels will sit. Mark for the dowels about 2 inches in from each panel end, staggering the dowels on the opposing faces of the legs so that the dowels won't intersect. *Note:* At this point you will be marking for two dowel holes on the back side only of each front leg; the front cross rails that go between the front legs will be attached later.

Attach a doweling jig (see page 41, Fig. 24) and, at the points marked in pencil on each leg, drill out two ½-inch-diameter holes ⁹⁄₁₆ inch deep. Next, in the top center of each leg, drill one ⁹⁄₁₆-inch-deep, ½-inch-diameter hole for attaching the tabletop.

The Panels

Cut the two 8x17-inch side panels and one 8x16-inch back panel from 1-inch-thick oak. As with other large pieces, you may have to make these from narrower oak pieces, and use biscuits to join them (see pages 42-44).

After assembling, gluing and allowing the panels to dry thoroughly, insert metal dowel centers into the dowel holes that were drilled in the legs, and press the legs and panels together. The doweling centers will leave a mark on the edges of the panels.

Drill ⁹⁄₁₆-inch-deep holes for ½-inch-diameter dowels in each of these locations. Then glue up and insert dowels into the back legs and the three panels (see Fig. 2). Assemble the side panels and back legs first, drawing them together using bar or pipe clamps (see page 26, Fig. 5). Be sure to wipe off any excess glue before it dries. After these leg-and-side-panel sections have dried completely, glue and attach them to the back panel. Then clamp the wood and let it sit until thoroughly dried. At this point, you should have a box-shaped assembly, with an open front and two legs. The front legs will be attached later.

The Cross Rails

There are eight cross rails in this table design, an upper set of four and a lower set of four. The cross rails serve three purposes. They stabilize the bed stand, they act as supports and guides for the drawers, and they trap the dust panels. There are two rails on each of the four sides. The cross rails on the sides and back of the bed stand are each joined to the panels they back onto with two 1-inch-long, ½-inch-diameter dowels each. (The front cross rails are joined to the two front legs by dowels of the same size inserted into the end grain

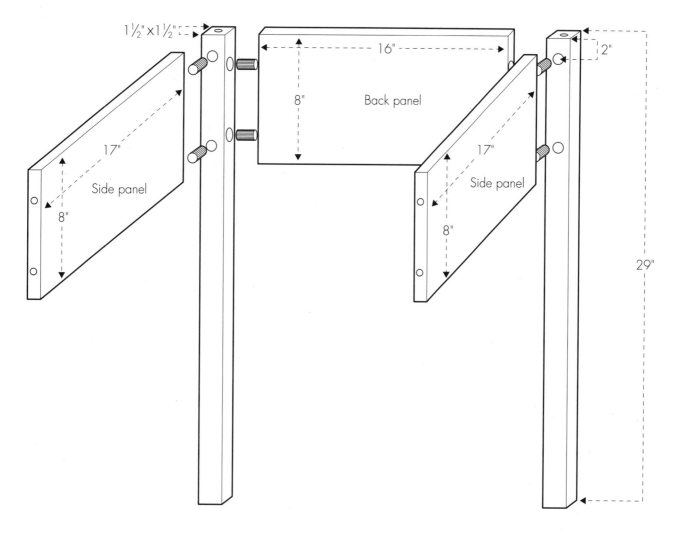

Fig. 2 *With the legs cut to length, drill dowel holes for the panels they will be joined to. Assemble the back legs, side panels and back panel.*

of the rails and into the side of the front legs.)

Before installing the rails, you have to prepare them for what Stickley called "dust panels." A dust panel keeps dust from falling from the underside of the upper drawer into the lower drawer, or from the underside of the lower drawer onto the floor. The panels in this bed stand are made of ⅜-inch birch plywood. To accommodate the dust panels, you have to cut a channel or dado on the inside edge of all the cross rails. It will save time and hassle if you rout this dust panel dado into *all* your 1-inch-thick rail stock *before* cutting it to the various rail

lengths. The dado width should match the thickness of your dust panel. If you choose ⅜-inch birch plywood as recommended here, rout out a ⅜-inch-wide dado with a straight bit loaded into your router. Make each dado ½ inch deep (see Fig. 3).

All the rails are the same dimension except for their lengths: The front rails are 16 inches long, but the side and back rail lengths depend on where you place the panels. (Fig. 3 shows them centered.) So, it makes the most sense to measure for the rails now, after the side and back panels have been joined to one another.

Also note that the vertical elevation of the rails has to leave room for the drawers. Rails that are too close together will bind the drawers; rails too far apart will make the drawers too loose. Since the

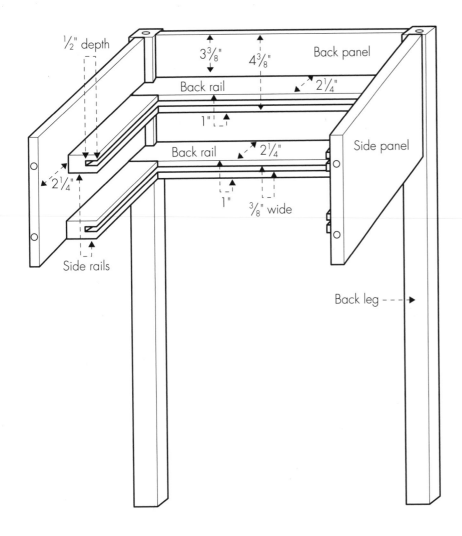

½" depth

3⅜"   4⅜"   Back panel

Back rail   2¼"

1"

Back rail   2¼"   Side panel

2¼"

1"   ⅜" wide

Side rails

Back leg - - - ➤

Fig. 3 *The back cross rails are notched to fit around the inside corners of the legs. With the rails in position and joined by dowels, you have a drawer support with routed channels into which the dust panels slide.*

out of the 1x2¼-inch oak that has been routed for the dust panels. (These rails will be about 16½ inches long.) Then measure the legs' protruding corner dimensions, and notch out that much on the ends of the two back rails with a jigsaw or a backsaw (¼ inch square). Next, on the back side of these two back rails, drill out two ½-inch-diameter, 9/16-inch deep holes, spacing them 2 inches in from each end, for the two dowels that will hold each rail in place.

To locate the rails' positions on the back panel, measure down from the top of the back panel the distance of the top drawer, or 3⅜ inches (see Fig. 3). Make a mark on the panel, then use a square to draw a line across the inside face of the back panel at this 3⅜-inch dimension. This will be the top of your upper back rail. Don't attach this upper rail just yet.

Next, to find where to install the lower rail, measure down from this upper rail line the thickness of your upper rail stock (1 inch), plus another 3⅜ inches (3¼ inches for the drawer height plus ⅛ inch to allow the drawer to slide). That puts the lower line, which must be square to the legs, 4⅜ inches below the first line you drew. It marks the top edge of the lower back rail (see Fig. 3).

Now you can install the rails. Insert dowel centers into the dowel holes you drilled in the backs of the rails. Hold the back rails, one at a time,

drawers are each 3¼ inches high, the rails have to accommodate them by leaving just that much space between them, plus ⅛ inch so the drawers won't bind—a total of 3⅜ inches. The upper rail will leave this much room between the top of the upper rail and underside of the tabletop; the lower rail will leave this much space between the top of the lower rail and the underside of the upper rail. (You may want to build your drawers ahead of time and use them as spacers to determine the placement of your rails.)

Cut the rails to length per your panel placement, starting with the back rails. First, measure the distance between the side panels, noting that the back rails will have to be notched for the back legs, as shown in Fig. 3. Cut two rails to this length against the back panel and press them against the back panel. The marks left by the dowel centers will be your guides for drilling the dowel holes. Use a ½-inch-diameter drill bit and make the holes ⁹⁄₁₆ inch deep. Now, glue and dowel these two rails to the back panel using the techniques described earlier in this book (see pages 41-42).

With the two back rails in place, use a square to draw reference lines on the side panels for the side rails. As for the lengths of these rails, their ends should be recessed back from the front edge of the side panels by 2¼ inches, or the width of the front rails (see Figs. 3 and 4). Cut them to length (14¼ inches), then drill out two ⁹⁄₁₆-inch-deep, ½-inch-diameter holes, each 2 inches in from the end, on the back of each side rail. Dowel and glue them in place just as you did the rails along the back panels.

Now it's time to join the front rails to the front legs. The two front rails are 16 inches long, but they must be doweled to the front two legs before the legs are attached to the panels. First, mark on the legs where the rails will go, measuring down 3⅜ inches for the top of the first rail, and from there another 4⅜ inches for the top of the lower rail. Dowel these rails into the *insides* of the front legs with the front of the legs flush with the front of the rails (you already have dowel holes in place on the *back* side of the front legs for the side panels). Use the techniques and dowel hole dimensions used on the other rails, but remember you are doweling into the *end grain* of the rails (see Fig. 4).

Assembling the Legs, Panels & Rails

The two 13¼x13¾-inch ⅜-inch plywood dust panels have to be inserted before the front rail-and-leg assembly is put in place. (You can't insert them after the rails are all in place because they are boxed in by the front rails.) Apply glue to the back and side edges of the dust panels, and slide them into

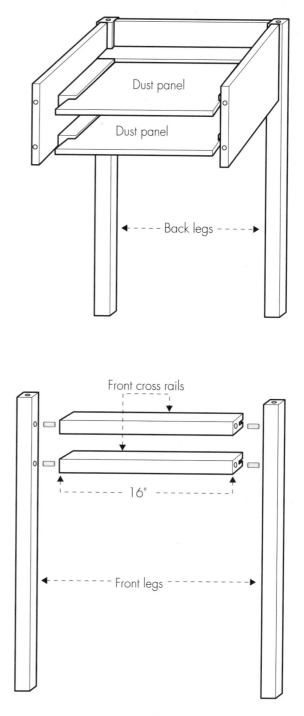

Fig. 4 *Insert the dust panels, then join the front rail-and-leg assembly to the side panels.*

place. Then attach the front legs to the side panels, gluing, doweling and clamping them in place. Let the assembly sit for an hour or so to let the glue set up before attaching the tabletop.

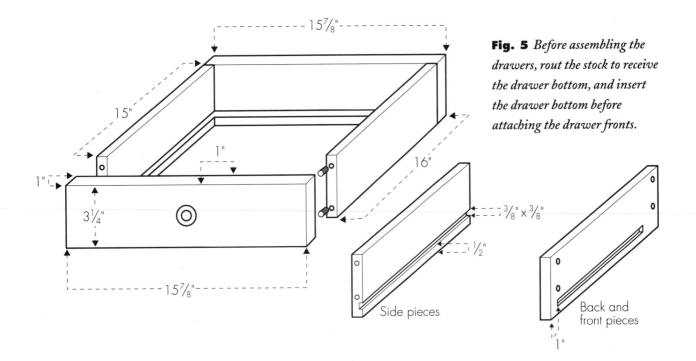

Fig. 5 *Before assembling the drawers, rout the stock to receive the drawer bottom, and insert the drawer bottom before attaching the drawer fronts.*

Side pieces

Back and front pieces

Attaching the Tabletop

To attach the tabletop, first insert dowel centers in the dowel holes that you drilled into the tops of the four legs (⁹⁄₁₆-inch-deep holes for 1-inch-long dowels). Next, position the tabletop, with an equal overhang to the left and right, and with the back edge of the tabletop flush with the back of the back panel. When you have it positioned, apply moderate downward pressure, so the dowel centers can leave their marks. Remove the tabletop, and drill holes for the dowels. Blow the dowel holes clean of sawdust, then apply glue to the dowels and along the top edge of the panels. Using bar or pipe clamps, draw the tabletop snug against the tops of the panels and legs.

The Drawers

The drawers can be simply butt-joined (see Fig. 5) with dowels to secure the joints. The assembled drawers will measure 3¼ inches high, 15⅞ inches wide and 17 inches deep (15-inch-long sides and 1-inch-thick fronts and backs). Before you assemble the drawer, cut a ⅜x⅜-inch routed channel ½ inch up from the bottom of the stock, so you can fit in a drawer bottom made of ⅜-inch birch plywood. For the side pieces of the drawer, rout this channel the full length of the drawer stock, but for the back and front pieces, stop the channel 1 inch short of the ends of the board (see Fig. 5).

After three sides of the drawer have been assembled (creating a box with an open front), slide in the bottom piece of 14¾x15¾-inch birch plywood, then glue, dowel and clamp the front piece on, using 1-inch-long, ½-inch-diameter dowels.

The knob on the front of each drawer can be oak, brass, wrought iron or whatever suits your fancy. A variety of knobs are available at cabinet shops or through woodworking supply catalogs.

Finishing the Bed Stand

After you have assembled the bed stand, sand it smooth, removing any pencil marks or blemishes that the piece has picked up during the assembly process. Then finish it as described on pages 47-53.

CHAPTER 8

Bookcase

The family circle who reads much nowadays wants to read intelligently, and this is only to be accomplished by convenient reference books; and books to be convenient must be close at hand.... The Craftsman encyclopedia bookcase is designed to meet just this condition, to furnish convenient reference to busy people without especial exertion." So states *The Craftsman* magazine in 1907 about this chapter's project. Stickley's words still ring true today. Even in the age of CD-ROMs and the Internet, there's still the need for a convenient place to use and store large-size reference books, such as an atlas, dictionary or encyclopedia.

With its simple joinery and cuts, this is an easy project for the intermediate woodworker and only mildly challenging for the beginner. No matter what your level of expertise, however, you'll be creating a truly satisfying piece, with classic Mission lines and features, like the poke-through tenons on the bottom shelf support and the half-moon curves cut into the bottom of the sides.

As with any woodworking project, the easiest way to approach the bookcase is to break it down into its component pieces, then cut and assemble each one.

The Sides

The sides of this bookcase are cut at an angle along the top so that they measure 50 inches along the back edge and 45 inches along the front. They are 12 inches wide, which means you will probably have to assemble them from narrower 1-inch-thick oak boards and join them with biscuits (see pages 42-44). After the sides have been assembled, glued and allowed to dry thoroughly, cut the tops at a 65-degree angle. To mark this angle, measure down 5 inches on the front side of the board and draw a line from that point to the top back corner. Cut along this line with a table saw (see Fig. 1).

CUT LIST AND MATERIALS

SIDES: (2) 1-inch-thick oak, 12x50 inches

BACK: (1) 1-inch-thick oak, 19x44 inches

SHELVES: (3) 1-inch-thick oak, 10x19 inches

RAILS: (2) 1x2-inch oak, 21 inches long

TOP: (1) 1-inch-thick oak, 14x21 inches

STOP FOR TOP: (1) 1½x1¾-inch oak,
   21 inches long

CLEATS: (2) 18-inch-long oak 2x2, ripped at
   65 degrees

DOWELS:
  (3) 1¼-inch-long, ¼-inch-diameter dowels
  (for the stop)

  (6) 1½-inch-long, ⅜-inch-diameter dowels
  (for the top)

  (4) 1-inch-long, ½-inch-diameter dowels
  (for the cleats)

DOWEL CENTERS:
  (6) ⅜-inch-diameter metal dowel centers

  (4) ½-inch-diameter metal dowel centers

GLUE: Yellow carpenter's glue

Next, load your router with a 1-inch straight bit and, starting at the top of one side board, make a 44-inch-long rabbet cut, ½ inch deep and 1 inch wide, along the back inside edge (see Fig. 1, Detail). Later, the back of the bookshelf will be attached here with a rabbet joint (see page 46).

Along the bottom edge of the side boards, mark and make a curved cut by following the instructions for curved cuts on page 45. The height and shape of the curve can be whatever appeals to you, but be sure it is centered so that the apex of the curve is at the center of the board, or 6 inches from both ends.

The Back

The 19x44-inch back piece does not extend all the way to the floor, but sits flush against the back of the bottom shelf. You will need to join together two or more narrower 1-inch-thick oak boards with biscuits to make this piece. After assembling the back, run it through your table saw, cutting the top edge at a 65-degree angle to match the angle of the top of the side boards. These angled edges should line up when the back and sides are in place (see Fig. 2).

The Shelves

The three shelves, also made from 1-inch oak boards, are 19 inches long and 10 inches wide. Each shelf is recessed 1 inch in from the front edge of the side pieces and is fit (and glued) into ½x1-inch dadoes or routed channels cut into the inside face of the side pieces.

To mark for the dadoes, measure up 5 inches from the bottom of the side board, and draw a line parallel to the bottom of the side board. This marks the bottom edge of the bottom shelf (see Fig. 2). Draw another line 1 inch above that to mark the dado that will be routed out to fit the shelf.

Next, from the top line of this first dado, measure up 12 inches (the distance between the shelves), and draw another parallel line. One inch above that, draw a fourth line to mark the middle dado. Repeat this procedure for marking the top dado.

Remember that each dado should be recessed 1 inch in from the front of the bookcase.

Once you have the dadoes marked, use a 1-inch straight bit in your router to make the ½-inch-deep dadoes (see page 29).

(continued on page 91)

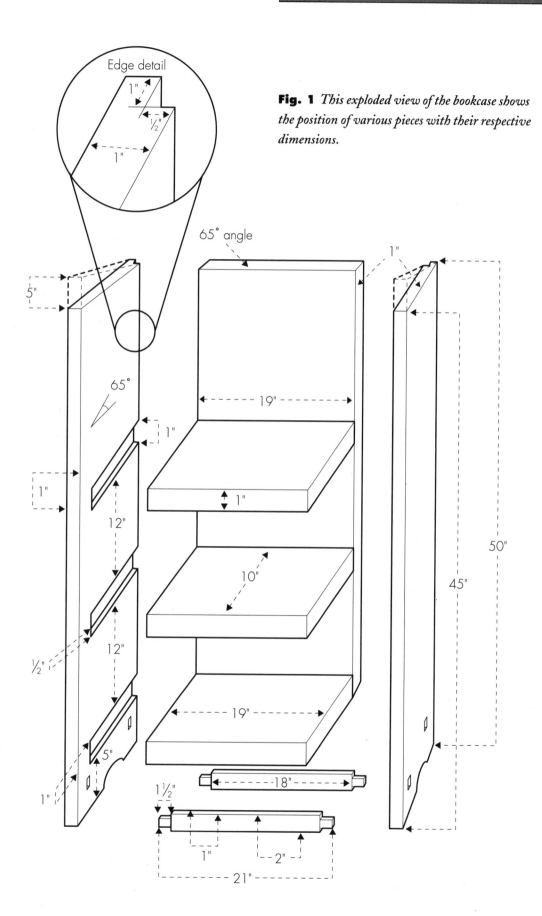

Edge detail

1"

½"

1"

Fig. 1 *This exploded view of the bookcase shows the position of various pieces with their respective dimensions.*

65° angle

1"

5"

65°

1"

1"

12"

19"

1"

10"

12"

19"

½"

5"

1"

1½"

18"

1"

2"

21"

50"

45"

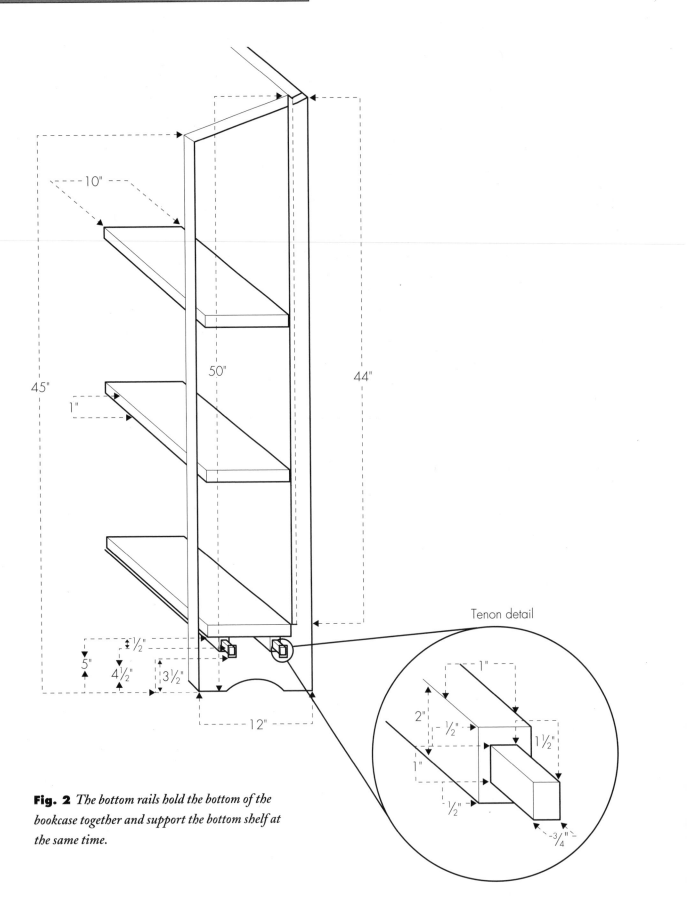

Fig. 2 *The bottom rails hold the bottom of the bookcase together and support the bottom shelf at the same time.*

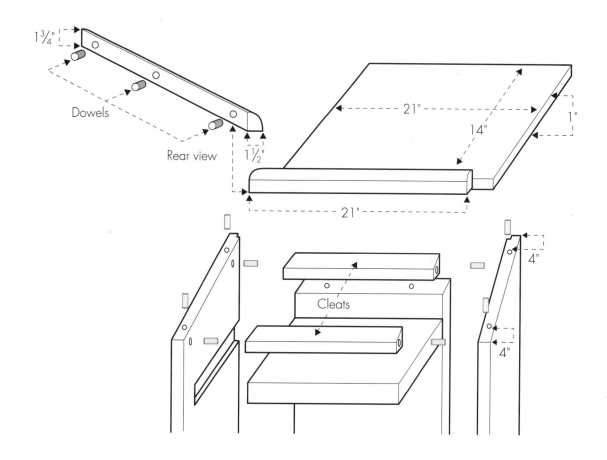

Fig. 3 *Two cleats are doweled into each side piece and into the back piece, holding the top end of the bookcase together and supporting the top piece.*

The Rails

Two rails support the lowest shelf, each with poke-through tenons at either end. The rails' shoulder-to-shoulder distance is 18 inches, but you must add onto that dimension 3 inches, the combined length of the 1½-inch-long tenons. That makes the rails a total of 21 inches long. To make them, you may have to mill down a larger piece of wood with your table saw and cut each rail so that it measures 1 by 2 by 21 inches.

The true tenons are milled out of the ends of the rails. Using the tenon-marking and tenon-cutting techniques introduced earlier (see pages 33-37), cut a tenon that is 1½ inches long, ¾ inch thick and has a ½-inch shoulder. The total rail length (including the tenons) should remain 21 inches.

Next, mark your mortises in the side boards. Since each tenon has a ½-inch shoulder, the top of each mortise will be ½ inch below the lower line of the bottom shelf channel. The mortise will have the same dimensions as the tenon, ¾ by 1 inch (see Fig. 2, Detail). Position the rails 3 inches in from the front and back.

The Top

The top of the bookcase is made from a 1-inch-thick piece of oak measuring 14 by 21 inches. You will have to assemble it from narrower 1-inch oak boards that are biscuit-joined together.

The top piece is attached to the sides and back of the bookcase using 1½-inch-long, ⅜-inch-diameter dowels (see Fig. 3) inserted into the end

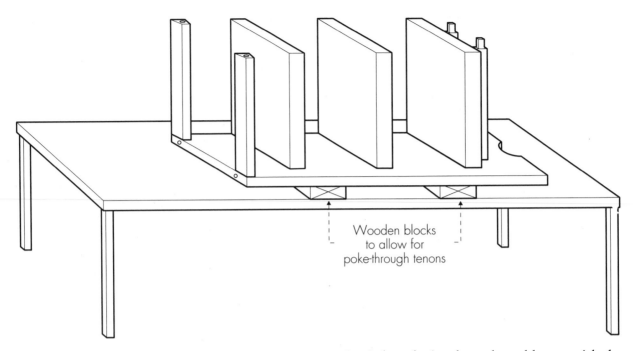

Wooden blocks
to allow for
poke-through tenons

Fig. 4 *When assembling the bookcase, lay it down on one side, resting on top of wooden blocks. Stand the unit upright, however, to attach the bookcase top piece.*

grain of the side boards and the end grain of the back. Use two dowels on each side board, and two dowels on the back, using a doweling jig (see page 41) to place a dowel 4 inches in from each board edge. Drill ⅜-inch-diameter holes 13/16 inch deep, which allows ¾ inch (half the dowel length), plus the 1/16 inch needed to accommodate excess glue.

Blow the drilled holes clean of sawdust, but don't insert the dowels yet. First, you'll need to assemble the other parts of the bookcase. Putting the top on is the last step, because you can't mark the location for the dowels in the top until the rest of the bookcase is assembled.

The Cleats

Extra support for the top is provided by two cleats (cross rails) that are doweled to the side boards and glued to the underside of the top piece when it is finally in place. To make these cleats, take 2-inch by 2-inch oak stock and rip it by run-

ning it lengthwise through a table saw with the blade set at 65 degrees, matching the angle on the top of the bookcase. Each cleat should be 18 inches long, but double-check this length on your bookcase, as it can change if the shelf dadoes are deeper or shallower than ½ inch. Drill for dowels in the bookcase sides and the end grains of the cleats (see Fig. 3), using the dowel-centering method explained earlier (see pages 41-42). Make each ½-inch-diameter hole 9/16 inch deep, to accommodate half the length of the 1-inch dowel, plus the excess glue.

Assembling the Bookcase

It is best to assemble the bookcase by laying it down on one side (see Fig. 4). To account for the poke-through tenon on the rails, set it on top of some scrap blocks of wood. Glue the shelves, rails and cleats and fit all the pieces into one side board.

Once these pieces are in place, with the glue still wet, glue up the ends and edges of these pieces and set the other side board down on top of the assembly. Gravity will hold this top side board in place while you get the back piece ready.

Place the back piece between the side boards and into the rabbet cut you routed out. Once the side boards, back, rails, cleats and shelves are in position and carefully aligned, use bar or pipe clamps (see page 26) to draw the assembly together. Wipe off any excess glue before it has a chance to dry.

Attaching the Top

Allow the bookcase to dry for at least one hour before you mark and drill the underside of the top piece for doweling. Stand the bookshelf up and insert doweling centers in the holes you already drilled for dowels in the top of the side boards and the back. Then lay the top of the bookcase in place, so that the back edge of the top is aligned properly and flush with the top of the back piece. Press down on the top piece.

Now remove the top piece and locate the dowel center marks on its underside. This is where you will drill the ⅜-inch-diameter holes. Because you can't attach a doweling jig to a board this wide, you'll have to freehand the dowel holes. With the bookcase top piece laying good side down on a work surface, hold your drill bit plumb and drill down ¹³⁄₁₆ inch.

After you clean out the dowel holes, glue up the dowels in the back and side pieces and set the top in place. Clamp the bookcase once more, using bar or pipe clamps (and blocks of wood, if necessary, to account for the angled top), and let the piece sit until the glue has dried thoroughly. Wipe off any excess glue immediately.

The Stop

A stop is attached to the bottom edge of the top piece to keep the book on display from sliding down the sloped surface. This piece is made from 1½x1¾-inch oak cut to a length of 21 inches. Round off its outside top corner (see Fig. 3) with a sander or a round-over bit from a router.

Attach the stop to the front edge of the top piece with ¾-inch-long brass screws or with three 1¼-inch-long dowels, depending on the look you prefer. Dowels are more authentic since very few Mission pieces used screws. (If you decide to use screws, be sure to predrill pilot holes for them.) The dowels will require ⅝-inch-deep, ¼-inch-diameter holes.

Once you have the entire piece assembled, sand and finish it according to the instructions outlined earlier (see pages 23-25 and 47-53).

CHAPTER 9

Coffee Table

This elegant coffee table is based on a classic Mission design and includes traditional details such as the narrow end slats and the arched cut on the underside of the bottom side braces. There is one feature, however, that borrows from a more contemporary style: the tabletop's tapered edge. This has been incorporated into the project instructions, but you can exclude this slight variation and keep the edges square if you prefer the more traditional look.

This Mission coffee table is a relatively difficult project, mainly because it involves mortising techniques for the end slats, which present a challenge to even the intermediate woodworker. The rest of the table, however, is put together with dowels.

Like any ambitious woodworking project, this one is easier to handle if you break it down into its component parts.

The Tabletop & Shelf

The tabletop is made from 1¼-inch-thick oak measuring 18 inches by 40 inches. You should have no problem finding oak stock 40 inches long, but you'll have to use biscuit-joining techniques (see pages 42-44) to glue up a piece 18 inches wide. You could use three 6-inch-wide boards, a combination of boards of varying widths that add up to 18

CUT LIST AND MATERIALS

TABLETOP: (1) 1¼-inch oak, 18x40 inches

LEGS: (4) 1¾x1¾-inch oak, 16 inches long

UPPER CROSS BARS: (2) ¾x2½-inch oak, 9½ inches long

LOWER CROSS BARS: (2) ¾x2½-inch oak, 9½ inches long

LENGTHWISE CROSS BARS: (2) ¾x2½-inch oak, 31½ inches long

SLATS: (6) ⅜x¾-inch oak, 10¾ inches long

SHELF: (1) ¾x7½-inch oak, 32½ inches long

BISCUITS: An assortment of #0 biscuits for joining the tabletop and shelf

DOWELS:
TABLETOP TO LEGS: (4) 1½-inch-long, ½-inch-diameter wood dowels

LEGS TO END CROSS BARS: (16) 1½-inch-long, ⅜-inch-diameter wood dowels

SHELF TO END CROSS BARS: (4) 1½-inch-long, ½-inch-diameter wood dowels

LEGS TO LENGTHWISE CROSS BARS: (8) 1½-inch-long, ⅜-inch-diameter wood dowels

GLUE: Yellow carpenter's glue

DOWEL CENTERS:
(8) ⅜-inch-diameter metal dowel centers
(4) ½-inch-diameter metal dowel centers

inches or glue up boards whose combined widths are greater than 18 inches and run the resulting piece lengthwise through your table saw to trim it down to size.

After assembling and gluing the boards together, clamp them with bar or pipe clamps (see page 26), and let them sit for at least an hour, or for the time recommended by the glue manufacturer. Be sure to wipe off any excess glue before it has a chance to dry. *Note:* If you prefer the tapered edge on your tabletop, postpone gluing and joining the boards until after you have made the cuts described in the next section.

The ¾x7½x32½-inch shelf should be easier to obtain. You may be able to find a single board with these dimensions, as a 1x8 has an actual dimension (¾ inch by 7¼ inches) very close to what you need. Or you can buy a 1x10 (¾ inch by 9¼ inches) and run it through your table saw to cut it down to the proper width.

Both the tabletop and the shelf are held in place by 1½-inch-long, ½-inch-diameter dowels.

Cutting the Tapered Edge

To cut the tapered edge on the tabletop, use a table saw with the saw blade set at a 33-degree angle, or whatever angle you prefer. It is difficult to cut this tapered edge once the tabletop is assembled, so you'll need to make this cut on the two outside boards before the pieces are joined together. To hold the boards in place for cutting, you may have to make a jig, using a 2x4 and a piece of plywood. Stand the 2x4 on edge, and screw through it into a piece of plywood that is about 10 inches tall. The jig should be as long as the stock you are running through the table saw (see Fig. 1).

With the jig assembled, first take some scrap wood that is the same thickness as your tabletop stock, and run it through the table saw, with the jig against the miter gauge of the saw. Check to see if you like the angle of the taper. If not, adjust the saw blade angle, and run through another piece of scrap wood; repeat this step until you get a taper to your liking. Then run your tabletop pieces

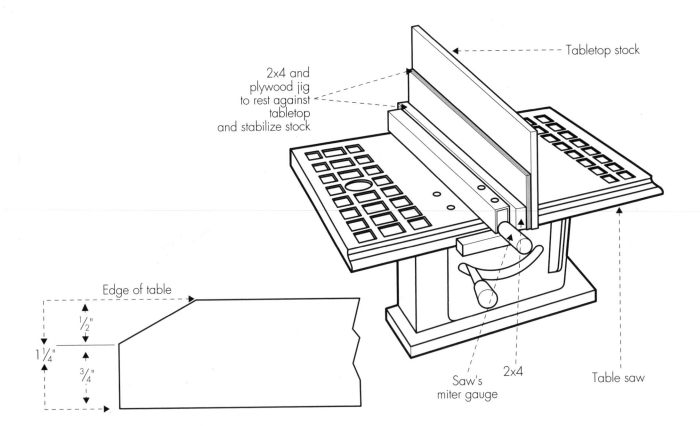

2x4 and plywood jig to rest against tabletop and stabilize stock

Tabletop stock

Edge of table

1/2"

1 1/4"

3/4"

Saw's miter gauge

2x4

Table saw

through the saw. Remember, if you are making these cuts on the component pieces of the tabletop, be sure you taper the edges that will be the outside top edges of the tabletop.

The End Pieces

Each of the two end pieces is made up of two legs, two cross bars and three slats. Each 1¾-inch-square leg is 16 inches long; each ¾x2½-inch cross bar is 9½ inches long; and each ⅜x¾-inch slat is 10¾ inches long.

Since the cross bar is ¾ inch thick, 1-by stock will suit you well here, as it is nearly ¾ inch or can be easily milled down. To get a width of 2½ inches, use your table saw to mill a piece of 1x3 stock down to size if necessary.

To get the ⅜x¾-inch slats, you'll have to run each one through your table saw, because this is such an odd size. Set your table saw's miter gauge at ⅜ inch, and run through some 1-by stock. The

Fig. 1 *To create a tapered edge on the tabletop, set your saw blade at the desired angle, and—using a plywood-and-2x4 brace—run the tabletop through the saw. It's easier to make this cut before the tabletop has been pieced together.*

resulting piece will have the required ⅜-inch thickness, but you may have to run it through again, with the miter gauge set at ¾ inch, to get the right width. When you have the stock cut to the right thickness and width, use your chop saw to cut six of these slats into 10¾-inch lengths.

Mortising & Doweling the End Pieces

Before the legs and cross bars can be joined together, the cross bars have to be mortised for the slats. The upper cross bar is mortised along its bottom edge; the lower cross bar is mortised along its top edge. Mark the locations for the ¾-inch by ⅜-inch mortises so they are ¾ inch apart from one another and 2⅞ inches in from the ends (see Fig. 2). Then, using a mortising bit on your drill press or a router loaded with a ⅜-inch straight bit (see page 29), rout out the mortises to a depth of about 1 inch (¹³⁄₁₆ inch to be exact—¾ inch plus ¹⁄₁₆ inch). Clean up the sides of the mortise with a sharp chisel, and blow them clean of sawdust.

After cutting the mortises for the slats, mark where the ⅜-inch-diameter dowel holes should be drilled into the ends of all four cross bars by measuring ¾ inch in from both edges. Use a doweling jig (see page 41) to center the dowels in the end grain (see Fig. 2), then drill them out using a ⅜-inch bit. Each hole should be ¹³⁄₁₆ inch deep (half as long as the 1½-inch dowel, or ¾ inch, plus ¹⁄₁₆ inch to accommodate excess glue).

On the *inside* face *of the two lower cross bars only,* mark where the two ½-inch-diameter holes should be positioned for the dowels that will hold the shelf in place. Mark 1½ inches down from the top edge and 2½ inches in from the ends, then drill all four holes out using a ½-inch-diameter drill bit. Plunge the drill bit into the stock only ⅜ inch, however, because the stock is only ¾ inch thick. (This is different from what was done on some other projects, where the dowel hole was half the length of the dowel. Here, since the dowel is 1½ inches long, you'll need to drill a hole 1⅛ inches deep into the end grain of the shelf when we finally prepare it for doweling.)

On the underside of the lower cross bars, mark and cut a shallow curve (see page 45 for instructions on this procedure). Although this design fea-

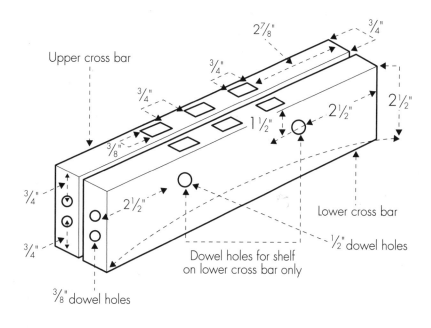

Fig. 2 *Use the dimensions shown here when cutting mortises for your end slats. Note, too, that the curved bottom and dowel holes should be marked and cut before the cross bars are attached to the legs.*

ture is characteristic of Mission furniture, you can eliminate it if you wish.

At this point, you should have four cross bars for the end pieces: two lower cross bars with curved cuts on their undersides (assuming you're including these cuts), ½-inch-diameter dowel holes on their inside faces for the shelf, ⅜-inch-diameter dowel holes on the ends for the legs, and slat mortises cut in the top edge; and two upper cross bars with ⅜-inch diameter dowel holes on the ends for the legs, and slat mortises cut in the undersides (see Fig. 2).

Milling & Drilling the Lengthwise Cross Bars

At this point, before the legs are doweled and attached to the end cross bars, it's time to mill the lengthwise cross bars and mark them for their at-

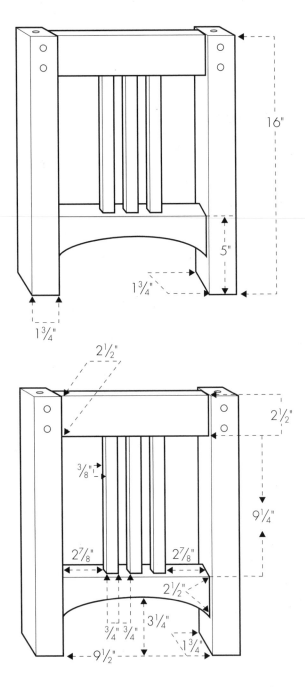

Fig. 3 *Drill dowel holes in the center tops of the legs where the tabletop will be attached. Refer to the dimensions given here when assembling the end pieces.*

tachment dowels to the legs. (This step is easier to do with the legs free.)

The lengthwise cross bars support the table along its length, and they are positioned perpendicular (90 degrees) to the end cross bars. Each ¾x2½x31½-inch cross bar is made from 1x3 oak stock (the same stock used in the end cross bars), milled down to size with your table saw if needed.

These lengthwise cross bars are attached to the legs with 1½-inch-long, ⅜-inch-diameter dowels, and positioned so their tops are flush with the tops of the legs. Using a doweling jig, mark and drill four ¹³⁄₁₆-inch-deep, ⅜-inch-diameter holes (two on both ends) in the end grain of each lengthwise cross bar. Center each hole ¾ inch in from the edge of the cross bar stock, as you did with the end cross bars (see Fig. 2).

Marking the Leg Dowels

Insert dowel centers into the just-drilled holes on the lengthwise cross bars and position the legs in place, to mark for the dowels that will attach the lengthwise cross bars to the legs. Insert metal dowel centers into the holes on the ends of the end cross bars to mark on the legs where to drill out for your leg-to-cross-bar dowels. With the top edge of the upper cross bar flush with the top edge of the legs, press the legs into the upper cross bar. Next, position the lower cross bar so it is 5 inches up from the bottom of the legs, and press the legs into the lower cross bar (see Fig. 3 for exact placement).

Doweling the Legs

You should now have six pinpoints marked in each leg for drilling the dowel holes. Because each dowel is 1½ inches long, this means drilling six ⅜-inch-diameter holes half as long as the dowel, or ¾ inch, plus ¹⁄₁₆ inch to accommodate excess glue, for a total of ¹³⁄₁₆ inch deep.

Next, use a doweling jig to mark and drill a ¹³⁄₁₆-inch-deep, ½-inch-diameter hole in the *top* of each leg, for doweling to the tabletop.

Hold off attaching any of the legs to any of the cross bars, because the slats have to be inserted first between the end cross bars.

Assembling the Slats, Cross Bars & Legs

Even though the slats have no real shoulder, you can still apply the "shoulder to shoulder" measurement concept here. The shoulder-to-shoulder measurement for the slats is 9¼ inches; that's how much of the slat you see revealed in the completed piece. The cut length for the slats is 10¾ inches, allowing 1½ inches for the "tenons": two times the mortise depth, ¾ on each end of the slat. Glue up the ends of each slat and insert them into the end cross bars, top and bottom. Draw the crosspieces together until the distance between them is 9¼ inches. Tightly clamp each cross bar assembly with bar or pipe clamps (see page 26), and let the glue set up for at least one hour, or for the glue manufacturer's recommended time. Wipe off any excess glue before it dries.

Once the slats are in place, glue and join the legs to the end piece assemblies (see Fig. 4). Clamp the legs to the cross bars using pipe or bar clamps, and let the glue dry the recommended time before going on.

Doweling the Shelf

With the end pieces securely assembled, insert dowel centers into the holes on the inside face of the lower cross bars. Position the shelf square to the lower cross bar, so the doweling centers leave their telltale mark in the center of the end grain of the shelf. Drill out four ½-inch-diameter holes, 1⅛ inches deep, two in both ends of the shelf.

Fig. 4 *This exploded view of an end piece shows how all its component pieces fit together.*

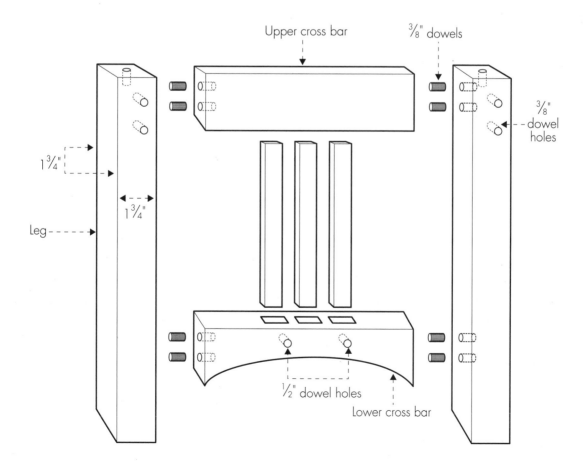

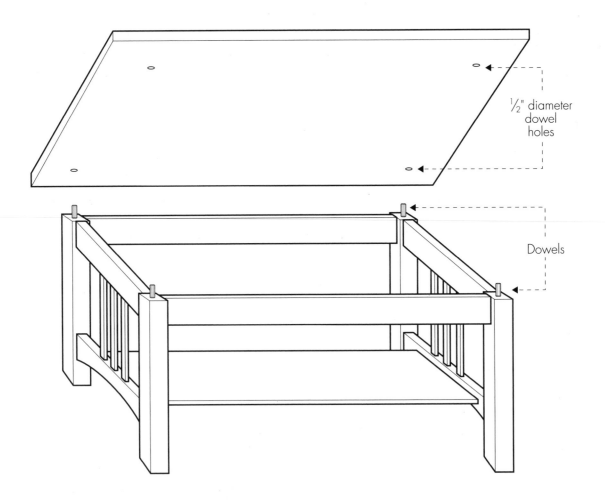

½" diameter
dowel
holes

Dowels

Assembling the Shelf & Lengthwise Cross Bars

The shelf and lengthwise cross bars have to be assembled all at once. Once the lengthwise cross bars are in place, all glued and clamped up, you can't attach the shelf. So the entire unit needs to be glued and clamped up simultaneously. This may be a two-person job, because you'll need to install the shelf, and then—before the end pieces are drawn tight against the shelf—hold the table assembly upright as the two lengthwise cross bars are installed. If you are working alone, set one end piece on the floor, inside face facing up, and install the lengthwise cross bar and shelf by standing them plumb and lowering the opposing end piece in place for clamping. (Be sure to install the shelf with glue

Fig. 5 *The tabletop should be attached last, using ½-inch-diameter dowels.*

not only on its dowels, as called for in any doweling connection, but with ample glue along its end grain where it joins into the end pieces.)

When all the pieces are doweled and glued up, draw the end pieces together using at least four clamps (bar or pipe clamps), one for each corner, so that the shelf and the lengthwise cross bars are all snugly held in place, and there are no gaps between any of the table's components.

The Tabletop

With the end pieces, shelf and lengthwise cross bars assembled, the tabletop can be put in position. But first you have to mark for the dowels that will hold it in place. Insert dowel centers in each of the four holes previously drilled in the tops of the four legs. Then set your tabletop in place, square it up to the ends and sides, and apply moderate pressure downward. The dowel centers will mark where to drill the ½-inch-diameter holes. Make each hole $^{13}/_{16}$ inch deep to accommodate half the length of the dowel plus $^{1}/_{16}$ inch for glue.

Apply glue to the dowels and along the top of all four cross bars, which should sit snugly up against the underside of the tabletop (see Fig. 5). Clamp the piece securely and let the finished table sit for 24 hours to allow the glue to completely set.

After the glue has dried, remove pencil marks, dirt or blemishes that may have marred the wood during assembly, and do a final sanding (see pages 23-25). Then finish the piece according to one of the methods described earlier (see pages 47-53).

CHAPTER 10

Magazine Table

This magazine table is a compact piece of furniture, which can be used unobtrusively in a number of household locations and for many more purposes than just holding magazines. It has classic Mission features, most notably the slats on the ends, and more subtly, the clean, square lines of the tabletop and legs.

This two-tiered table is a relatively easy piece to cut and assemble, with only two challenging aspects: the dado cuts on the legs where the shelf fits, and the sequence of assembly, which requires having a number of pieces already lined up before the tabletop is positioned and attached. But like any of the projects presented here, it gets easier when you take the process step-by-step.

The Tabletop & Shelf

The tabletop measures 18 inches by 35½ inches and can be made up of four 1-inch-thick, 4½-inch-wide boards cut to the required length. Using the biscuit-joining method (see pages 42-44), assemble the tabletop, clamp it together, then set it aside to dry thoroughly (see Fig. 1). Wipe off any excess glue before it dries. (Each board does not have to be the same width; use any combination of widths as

CUT LIST AND MATERIALS

TABLETOP: (1) 1x18x35½-inch oak piece

SHELF: (1) 1x16x30¾-inch oak piece

SLATS: (4) ½x2-inch oak, 10 inches long

LEGS: (4) 2x2-inch oak, 30 inches long

DOWELS: (4) 1½-inch-long, ½-inch-diameter wood dowels

GLUE: Yellow carpenter's glue

BISCUITS: An assortment of #0 biscuits for joining the tabletop and shelf

DOWEL CENTERS:
(4) ½-inch-diameter metal dowel centers

PEGS: 1¼-inch-long, ⅜-inch-diameter oak pegs (optional)

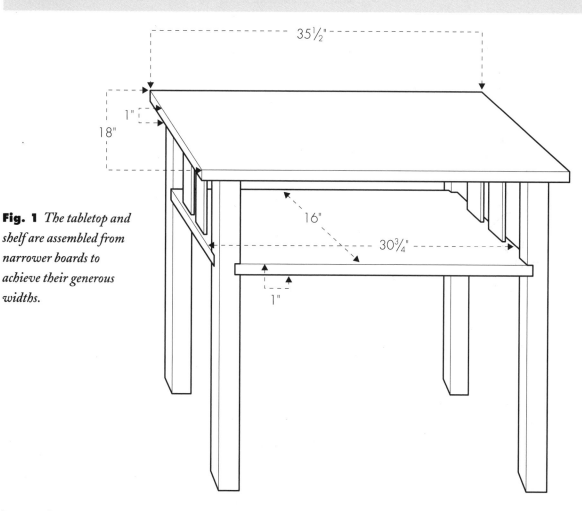

Fig. 1 *The tabletop and shelf are assembled from narrower boards to achieve their generous widths.*

long as the measurement equals 18 inches.)

Make the shelf next. This assemblage of boards, measuring 16 inches by 30¾ inches, can be made from four 1-inch-thick, 4-inch-wide boards cut to size and joined together with biscuits. As with the tabletop, after clamping the pieces together, wipe off any excess glue, then set the shelf aside to dry.

The Slats

Cut four slats to measure ½ inch by 2 inches by 10 inches. Each end of each slat will protrude ½ inch into a routed mortise, either one cut on the underside of the tabletop or one in the top side of the shelf. Though these slats don't have real shoul-

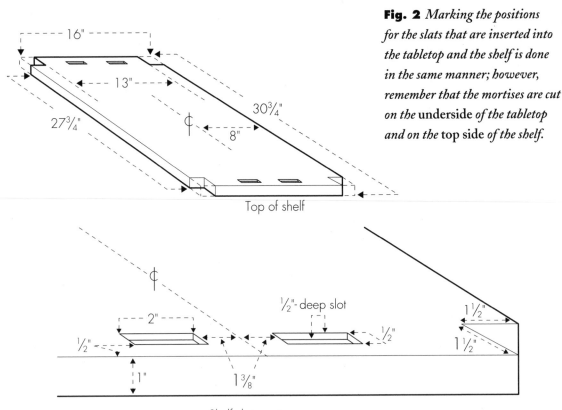

Fig. 2 *Marking the positions for the slats that are inserted into the tabletop and the shelf is done in the same manner; however, remember that the mortises are cut on the* **underside** *of the tabletop and on the* **top side** *of the shelf.*

Top of shelf

Shelf slat mortises

ders, the exposed portion of each slat measures 9 inches. So their "shoulder-to-shoulder" distance can be described as 9 inches.

Referring to the mortising techniques given earlier (see pages 34-36), mark out guidelines for your router for each of the mortises you will cut in the shelf and the tabletop. Each mortise should measure ½ inch wide, ½ inch deep and 2 inches long. To position them, find the center line of the shelf, and measure out 1⅜ inches to either side of this line and ½ inch in from the outside edges of the shelf (see Fig. 2). Since the slats are ½ inch thick, choose a straight router bit that leaves a ½-inch mortise and cut each mortise according to your marked guidelines.

Mark and cut corresponding slots in the underside of the tabletop. Again, find and mark the center of the tabletop, then use the same off-center dimensions to match the slat cuts below.

The Legs

Cut the four table legs from the 2x2-inch wood to a length of 30 inches. Next, using a router, a dado blade on a table saw or with repeated passes on your table saw, make the dado cuts into which the lower shelf will fit. The dado should be exactly as wide as the shelf itself (1 inch), the top of the cut should be 9 inches from the top end of the table leg, and the depth of the cut should be ½ inch (see Fig. 3). Make these cuts from two directions (on two adjoining sides), effectively cutting away the inside corner of the leg.

Next, use a doweling jig to drill a ½-inch-diameter hole 1 inch deep in the center of the top of each leg (see pages 40-42). If you don't have a doweling jig, use a drill with a level to make sure your drill hole is perfectly plumb.

One leg, three views

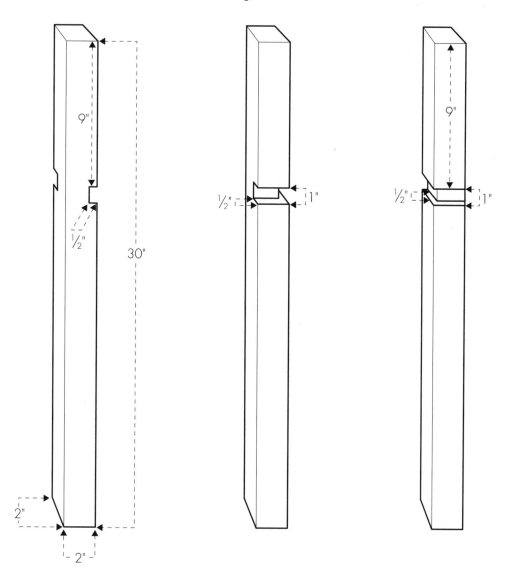

Fig. 3 *Each leg is cut identically with a dado on two adjoining sides.*

Cutting the Shelf Corners & Attaching the Legs & Slats

All four corners of the shelf will need to be notched so that they fit into the dado cuts on the legs. Since the dadoes are ½ inch deep, cut out a 1½x1½-inch corner notch (see Fig. 2) that leaves the shelf protruding just ½ inch into each leg. This makes the edge end-to-end length measurement 27¾ inches. The end-to-end width measurement of the shelf with the notch cut out is 13 inches (see Fig. 2). Use a jigsaw or saber saw for these cuts, and be careful not to overrun your cut lines. (Overrun cut lines would be visible after the table is assembled.)

Glue and clamp the shelf to the legs, and glue and insert the slats into the shelf (see Fig. 4). Wipe off any excess glue, then let the assembly dry for

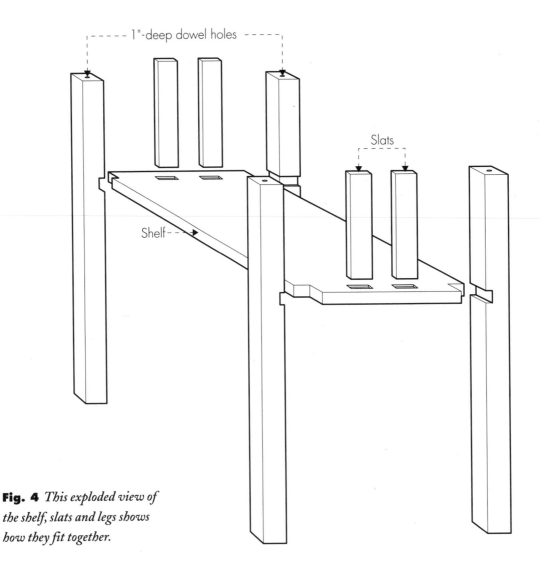

1"-deep dowel holes

Slats

Shelf

Fig. 4 *This exploded view of the shelf, slats and legs shows how they fit together.*

at least one hour, or for the manufacturer's recommended time.

Attaching the Tabletop

Before setting the tabletop in place on the shelf-leg-slat assembly, insert four ½-inch-diameter dowel centers in the legs' dowel holes. Then carefully place the tabletop on the legs so that it overhangs by 1 inch on all sides. When the tabletop is properly positioned, apply light downward pressure to set the dowel centers. Remove the tabletop, and, using a ½-inch-diameter drill bit, drill ½-inch-diameter holes that are only ½ inch

deep. Remember, the tabletop stock is only 1 inch thick: Use extra care so you don't poke through the other side. Next, lay the tabletop down with its routed slots and dowel holes facing up and apply glue into those areas.

Glue and insert dowels in the tops of the legs. Turn the shelf-leg-slat assembly upside down and put it on top of the underside of the tabletop (see Fig. 5). Insert the dowels, and drive the assembly together squarely with a rubber mallet, or draw it together with bar or pipe clamps (see page 26). Wipe off any excess glue before it dries on the wood, and leave the clamps in place until the glue is completely dry.

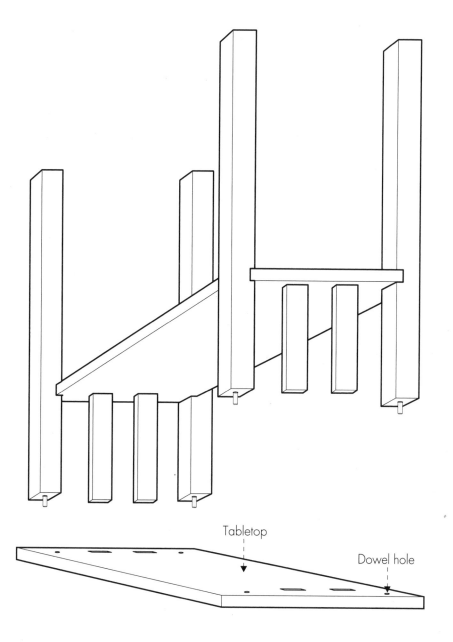

Tabletop

Dowel hole

A handsome addition to this table is pegging the joints where the shelf meets the legs. To do this, follow the instructions on pages 38-39, using ⅜-inch-diameter, 1¼-inch-long oak pegs. Drill four ⅜-inch-diameter, 1¼-inch-deep pilot holes, one per leg, and hammer in oak pegs centered in the leg-to-shelf joint. Trim the pegs with a backsaw, and sand them flush with the leg.

Once you have completely assembled the table, let it stand for 24 hours to allow the glue to dry

Fig. 5 *Attach the tabletop by placing it face down on a work surface and lowering the leg-slat-shelf assembly onto it.*

thoroughly. Remove any pencil marks or blemishes the table may have picked up during assembly, and sand it according to the directions on pages 23-25. Then refer to pages 47-53 to decide on and apply the finish of your choice.

CHAPTER II

Dining Table

This Mission dining table makes an exquisite, eye-catching centerpiece for any dining room. The table's clean, square lines, box stanchion and trademark Mission base configuration make it a true classic. It looks far more challenging to build than it actually is. If you break it down into its component parts, and complete each one in order, this project is a very manageable task. The dining table requires intermediate-to-advanced carpentry and joinery skills, so you may want to complete one or two of the easier projects in this book before taking it on.

The Tabletop

The 46-inch-square tabletop is assembled from narrower pieces of 1-inch-thick oak, cut to a length of 46 inches and joined together with biscuits (see Fig. 1A, and pages 42-44). You can join eight 6-inch-wide or four 12-inch-wide pieces of 1-inch oak, and trim the last piece as required. Or you can use boards of varying widths. However you assemble the tabletop, its final dimensions should be 46 inches square.

Attached to the underside of the tabletop is a

CUT LIST AND MATERIALS

TABLETOP: (1) 1-inch oak, 46x46 inches

FRAME BOX: (4) ¾x3-inch oak, 44 inches long

CLEATS: (8) 1½x1½-inch blocks, 4 inches long

ANCHOR BLOCKS: (2) 1x6x8-inch oak

POST:
(2) ¾x6-inch oak, 24 inches long
(2) ¾x8-inch oak, 24 inches long

BASE: (1) 1-inch oak, 10x12 inches

TABLE SUPPORT: (1) 1-inch oak, 8x30 inches

FEET:
(4) 3x3-inch oak, 5 inches long
(4) 3x3-inch oak, 14 inches long

FEET BLOCKS: (4) 1-inch-thick 4x4-inch oak blocks

BISCUITS: An assortment of #0 biscuits for joining the tabletop

SCREWS:

TABLETOP FRAME: (8) 1½-inch #8 wood screws and oak plugs

CLEATS: (24) 2-inch #8 wood screws

POST: (12) 2-inch #8 wood screws and oak plugs

BASE: (6) 2½-inch #8 wood screws

"T" TABLE SUPPORT: (6) 2½-inch #8 wood screws

FOOT TO FOOT: (8) 2½-inch #8 wood screws

FOOT TO BASE: (8) 2½-inch #8 wood screws

BLOCK TO FOOT: (4) 2½-inch #8 wood screws

ANCHOR BLOCKS TO TABLETOP: (8) 1½-inch #8 wood screws

"T" TO TABLETOP ANCHORS: (6) 2-inch #8 wood screws

GLUE: Yellow carpenter's glue

44-inch-square frame box border made of ¾x3-inch oak (see Fig. 1B). You can cut these pieces from 1x4 oak stock (measuring ¾ inch by 3½ inches), trimmed to a 3-inch width. Using a chop saw, cut the ends at a 45-degree angle to make a clean, mitered corner. Glue and screw this frame together, with two countersunk screw holes per corner, using 1½-inch #8 wood screws. Cover the screw heads with oak plugs (see Fig. 1B and pages 27-28). Be sure to predrill the oak, otherwise it will split (see page 27). As soon as the frame is assembled, wipe off any excess glue before it dries.

After the glue has dried the amount of time recommended by the manufacturer (usually about one hour), place the tabletop, good side down, on the floor, which has been covered with a cloth or tarp so as not to mar the top surface of the table. Apply glue to the top edges of the frame and set it, glued side down, on top of the table, centering it so it is equidistant from the tabletop edges on all four sides. Next, glue and screw 1½x1½x4-inch oak cleats (two per corner) into the tabletop, using one 2-inch #8 wood screw per cleat (see Fig. 2). Then drive two more 2-inch #8 wood screws horizontally through each cleat and into the inside faces of the frame. Remember to predrill all holes.

The Post & Base

The post that supports the tabletop is essentially a 24-inch-tall box, measuring 6 inches by 8 inches. The four pieces that make up the box are mitered together at 45-degree angles along their long edges (see Fig. 3). To get these angles, run each piece through your table saw with the blade set at 45 degrees. (If you don't feel confident about

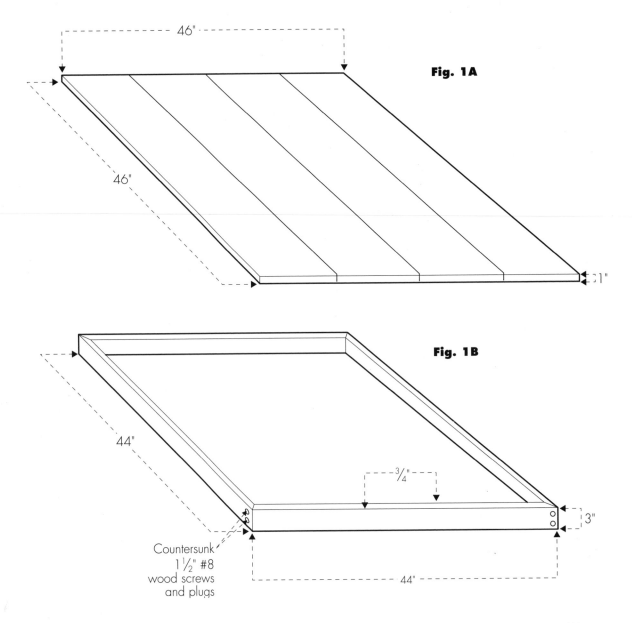

Fig. 1A

46"

46"

1"

Fig. 1B

44"

$\frac{3}{4}$"

3"

44"

Countersunk
1$\frac{1}{2}$" #8
wood screws
and plugs

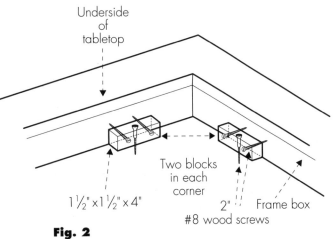

Underside
of
tabletop

Two blocks
in each
corner

1$\frac{1}{2}$" x 1$\frac{1}{2}$" x 4"

2"
#8 wood screws

Frame box

Fig. 2

Fig. 1A & 1B *The 46-inch-square tabletop* (A) *is assembled from narrower boards that are glued and joined together with biscuits. A frame with mitered corners* (B) *is fastened with countersunk screws and plugged.*

Fig. 2 *Attach the frame to the underside of the tabletop using two wooden cleats per corner. Screw through the cleats and into the underside of the table and then through the cleats into the inside face of the frame.*

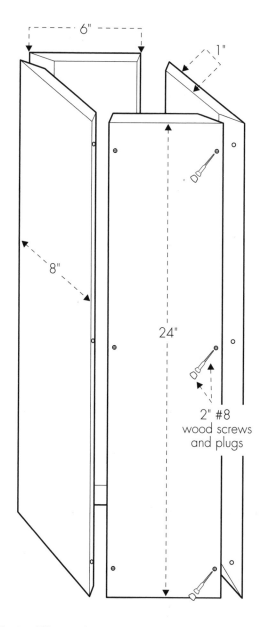

Fig. 3 *The post is assembled from four boards, ripped at 45 degrees along their long edges. Countersunk and plugged screws, three to a side, hold the boards together.*

making these cuts accurately, you can simply join the boards square, without the miters. Simply sandwich the 6-inch-wide boards between the 8-inch-wide boards, making the edges flush. But if you do this, add 2 inches to the width of your base, making it 12 inches instead of 10 inches.)

To assemble the post, apply glue to the angled faces (or overlapped portion on each board) and

clamp the assembly together with corner clamps (see page 26). Wipe off any excess glue as you go. Next, countersink three 2-inch #8 wood screws in each joint (see Fig. 3), and cover each of the recessed screw heads with oak plugs. Once the glue has dried, cut the tops of the plugs flush with the face of the wood using a backsaw (see page 39).

The base on which the post sits is nothing more than a 10x12-inch piece of 1-inch oak (see Fig. 4). This will probably have to be assembled from narrower pieces joined together with biscuits. Glue and assemble these pieces, then clamp them together and set the base aside while the glue dries. Wipe off any excess glue.

Assembling the Base, Post & Table Support

Glue and screw the post to the base with six 2½-inch #8 wood screws. You will be drilling up from what will be the underside of the post base. Countersink these screws so the screw heads will be recessed and won't scratch the floor. (There is no need to plug these countersunk holes.) As before, predrill for the screws.

With the base secured to the post, attach the table support to the top of the post. This table support will not be visible because the frame box border will hide it, but it is still best to use oak here if you can afford it, as the screws may tear out of a softer wood such as pine.

The "T" table support is an 8x30-inch piece of 1-inch oak. It sits squarely on top of the 8-inch-wide sides of your post. Attach the support to the top of the post with glue and six 2½-inch-long #8 wood screws (see Fig. 4). When you drive these screws down into the top of the post, you will be doing so blindly, as you can't see the post below. Without pencils lines to guide your drill placement, you may miss the post entirely or, worse, blow out a side of it with a screw that just misses.

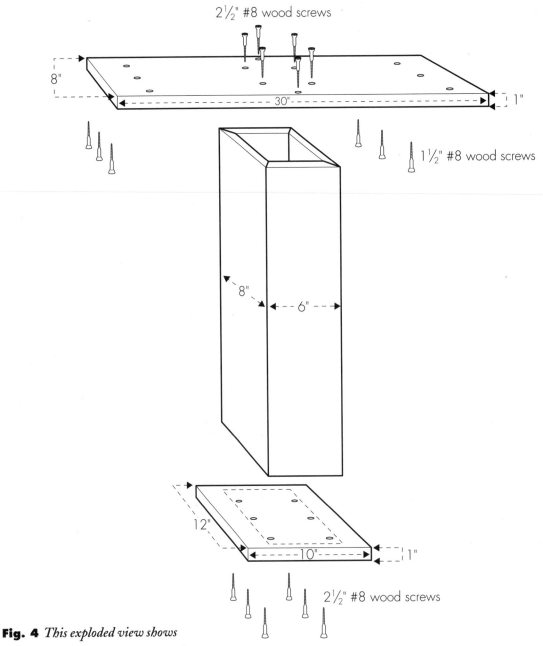

Fig. 4 *This exploded view shows how the base, post and "T" fit together.*

To avoid errant screw placement, place the post *on top* of the support board, positioned just as it will be when it is in place *under* the support board, and draw guidelines along the outside of the box to indicate the outer border of the "safe zone" in which to drive screws. Then return the post to its position under the support board, and—using the safe zone lines—drive the screws down into the top of the post.

Before attaching the tabletop to the T-support, glue and screw two anchor blocks (1x6x8-inch pieces of oak) to the underside of the tabletop (see Fig. 6), placing a 1½-inch #8 wood screw in each corner of the blocks as shown. The blocks will serve

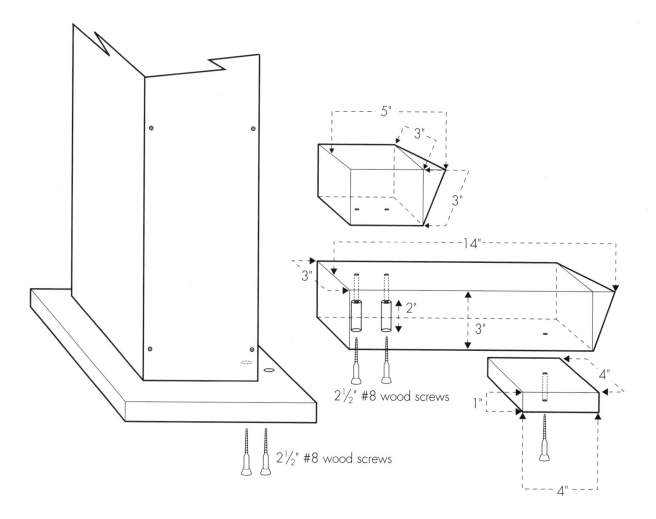

2½" #8 wood screws

2½" #8 wood screws

as the attachment point of the T-support to the tabletop. Note that in the drawing of the finished project (see page 108) the table does not align squarely with the post—it sits catty-corner to it. So when you position the anchor blocks, the "T" should position the post catty-corner to the tabletop. To find the exact anchor block location, set the tabletop over the T-support *without* the anchor blocks in place, then trace a guideline around the top of the T.

Be careful to choose the right length screw when attaching these blocks to the underside of the tabletop. If you use screws over 2 inches long, you risk going *through* the tabletop and ruining it. Since the blocks are 1½ inches thick and the tabletop is 1 inch thick, use 2-inch #8 wood screws to join them. Predrill as required.

Fig. 5 *The feet are secured to the base by screws that run up from the bottom of the base. Both the long and the short feet are detailed with a four-sided "pyramid" tip.*

Before attaching the tabletop to the T-support, you first need to attach the "feet" to the base and the post.

The Feet

There are eight feet on this table: four long ones that support and stabilize the base, and four short ones that serve as decoration (see Fig. 5).

The ends of the feet are all cut the same, with four 45-degree angles. (For instructions on how to make these angled cuts, refer to that part of the

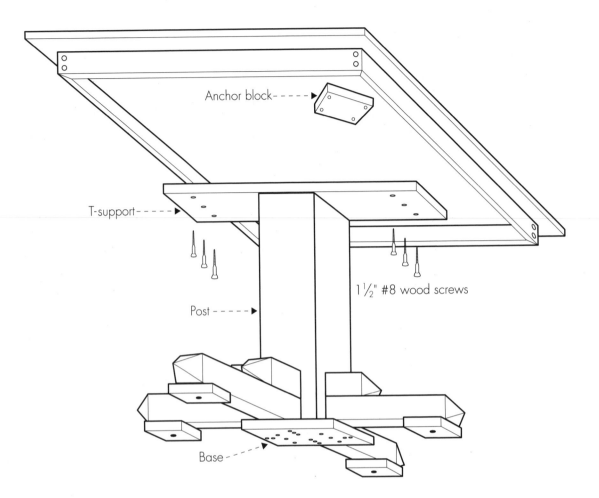

Anchor block- - - - -

T-support- - - - -

1½" #8 wood screws

Post - - - - -

Base - - -

wastepaper basket project, pages 61-63.) The feet pieces are held to each other with screws, and the feet assembly is attached to the base with screws that come up from the bottom.

The shorter feet are each 3 inches by 3 inches and 5 inches long. The length is measured from the square cut where the feet meet the post to the apex of the pyramid cut at the opposite end.

The longer feet are also 3 inches by 3 inches, but 14 inches long. Again, the length is measured from the square cut where the feet meet the post to the apex of the pyramid cut at the opposite end.

Using carpenter's glue at the joint, mount the short feet on top of the long feet with two 2½-inch #8 screws per set of feet. Since the lower (and longer) feet, through which you start the screws, are 3 inches thick, you would have to drive a 5-inch-long screw to attach the two feet components

Fig. 6 *You should be especially careful when screwing the two anchor blocks to the underside of the tabletop, so that the screws don't poke through to the top surface. The same applies when attaching the post and base unit to the anchor blocks.*

properly. Instead, you'll drill a larger hole halfway into the lower foot stock and start your screw there, recessing the screw into the lower foot. To do this, drill 2 inches into the underside of the longer feet stock with a ⅜-inch bit. This will allow room for the head of the screw, and when it is driven into the shorter foot, the screw will extend 1½ inches up into the short foot stock. After you have drilled with the ⅜-inch bit, you will need to predrill the rest of the way for the #8 screw itself, using the predrill techniques and bit size recommended earlier.

After you have glued and screwed the four sets of two feet together, attach them to the base, centered on the faces of the posts, by gluing and screwing up from the underside of the posts with two 2½-inch #8 wood screws per set of feet. Be sure to predrill for these screws to avoid splitting the hardwood, staggering the screws so they're off-center, and countersink them so the heads are recessed off the floor. There is no need to plug these countersinks; the countersinking just keeps the screw heads from scratching the floor.

Next, on the underside of each of the long feet, at the pointed end, install a 4x4-inch oak block, 1 inch thick (see Fig. 5). This will make contact with the ground, allowing the long feet to serve as outriggers to stabilize the table. Glue and screw these blocks to the underside of the feet with countersunk holes and using 2½-inch #8 wood screws. Again, there is no need to plug them, as you simply want to recess the screw heads so they don't scratch the floor.

Attaching the Tabletop

When you have the post, "T", base and feet assembled, attach this section to the underside of the table by screwing 2-inch #8 wood screws through the T-support and into the anchor blocks on the underside of the tabletop as shown (see Fig. 6). Be sure to predrill all holes. *Don't* glue these T-to-block joints, as you may want to remove the tabletop someday when moving the table from room to room.

When you have assembled your table, let it sit for 24 hours to allow the glue to completely dry. Then sand it as described earlier (see pages 23-25), and apply a finish of your choice (see pages 47-53).

CHAPTER 12

Morris Chair

The Morris chair was (and remains) so popular that Stickley's magazine *The Craftsman* presented Morris chair plans after "a number of requests for a Morris chair [design] that could be made at home." This particular one has poke-through leg tenons adorning the arms. Notice, too, the narrow slats between the arms and the seat frame, and the classic, square, clean lines of the legs and the back. This is an ambitious project that requires a great deal of patience, accuracy and skill. It is really for those with advanced woodworking skills who also have a well-equipped shop with a full range of power and hand tools (see pages 25-31).

The Legs & Rails

The chair legs are made from 2½-inch-square oak, each cut to a length of 21 inches. To get wood of this dimension, you may have to custom-order it.

To prepare the legs, make square cuts on the bottoms, and cut tenons in the tops (see pages 36-37). The tenons should be 2 inches high and 1½ inches square, with ½-inch shoulders (see Fig. 1, Leg tenon). If you want, finish the tops of the tenons with the four-sided pyramid, or chamfered, cuts (see pages 41-42 for details).

Cut the rails next. The front and two side rails measure 1½ inches by 5½ inches by 27 inches. The back rail measures 1½ inches by 3½ inches by 27 inches. The front and two side rails have tenons that are 2 inches long, 3½ inches high and ¾ inch thick, with 1-inch shoulders (see Fig. 1, A, B & C tenons). This gives a shoulder-to-shoulder measurement of 23 inches.

The back rail tenon is 2 inches long, 2½ inches high and ¾ inch thick, with a ½-inch shoulder (see Fig. 1, D tenon). Its shoulder-to-shoulder measurement is also 23 inches. (When you insert the side

CUT LIST AND MATERIALS

LEGS: (4) 2½x2½-inch oak, 21 inches long

SIDE AND FRONT RAILS: (3) 1½x5½-inch oak, 27 inches long

BACK RAIL: (1) 1½x3½-inch oak, 27 inches long

SLATS: (14) ¾x1¼-inch oak, 7½ inches long

ARMS: (2) 1¼x5-inch oak, 38 inches long

BACK STILES: (2) 2x2-inch oak, 31 inches long

BACK RAILS: (3) ¾x3-inch oak, 19¾ inches long

BACK SUPPORT: (1) 1¼x1½-inch oak, 27 inches long

BACK PINS: (2) 1-inch-diameter dowels, 6 inches long

CLEATS: (4) 1x1-inch oak, 23 inches long

SCREWS: (16) 2-inch #8 wood screws for seat cleats

SPACERS/WASHERS: (1) ½-inch-thick brass washer for 1-inch dowel

PLYWOOD: (1) ¾-inch plywood, 23x23 inches (notched at corners to fit seat)

FOAM: (1) 5-inch-thick foam, 23x23 inches (to match plywood)

LEATHER, NAUGAHYDE OR FABRIC: 3 yards total for cushions

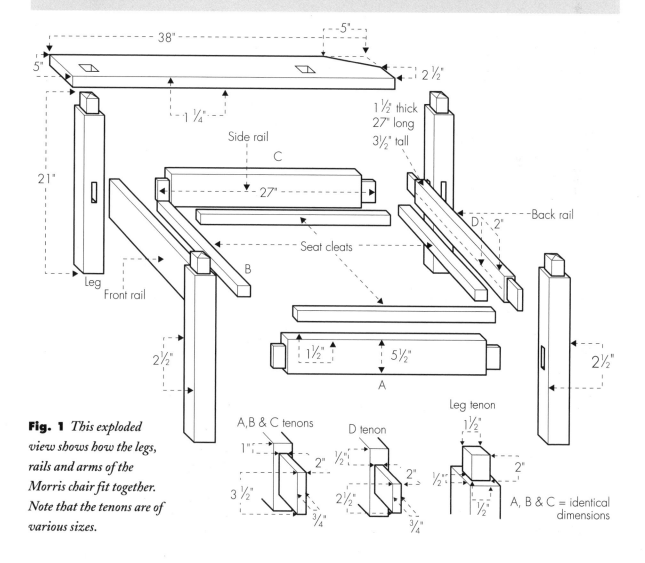

Fig. 1 *This exploded view shows how the legs, rails and arms of the Morris chair fit together. Note that the tenons are of various sizes.*

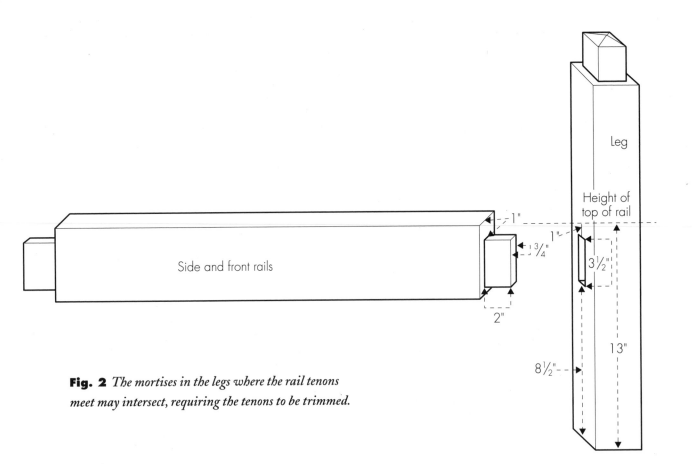

Fig. 2 *The mortises in the legs where the rail tenons meet may intersect, requiring the tenons to be trimmed.*

rails into the leg mortises, you'll find that one tenon will insert the entire 2 inches, but the adjoining rail tenon may be too long and need trimming.)

Referring to the dimensions in Fig. 1, cut all four rails.

Cutting Mortises to Receive Rails

The tops of the rails should be 13 inches above the ground. Since the shoulders on the side and front rails are each 1 inch, use a marking gauge to draw the top horizontal line for the leg mortises at 12 inches. Once this line is established, you can draw the rest of the mortise lines. Each mortise should be centered along this horizontal reference line and should be ¾ inch thick, 3½ inches high and 2 inches deep. Their base lines will be 8½ inches up from the bottom of the leg (see Fig. 2). If

you are using a router, load it with a ¾-inch straight bit. For drill press setup, use a ¾-inch mortising bit.

The back rail is narrower than the other three (3½ inches instead of 5½) because it needs to accommodate the back rest as it pivots on wooden pins. When positioning this rail, its *bottom* edge should line up with the bottom edges of the side rails. Since the bottom of the side rails are 7½ inches up from the ground, and the tenons on the back rail have a ½-inch shoulder, the bottom edge of the back rail mortise will start 8 inches up from the bottom of the leg. Use your marking gauge to draw guidelines from this reference point. These mortises should also be ¾ inch thick, 2½ inches high and 2 inches deep. If you are using a router, load it with a ¾-inch straight bit. For drill press setup, use a ¾-inch mortising bit.

Postpone assembling these pieces until the mortises for the slats have been cut.

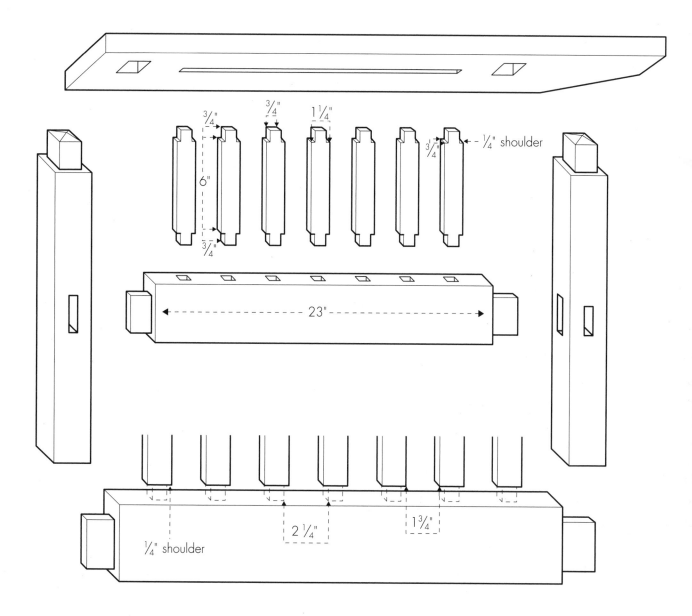

The Slats

The slats extend from the underside of the arms to the top of the side rails, with a shoulder-to-shoulder measurement of 6 inches. Using the ¾x1¼-inch oak, cut 14 slats, each to a length of 7½ inches. On the ends of each slat, cut a tenon that is ¾ inch long and ¾ inch high, with a ¼-inch shoulder. The tenon thickness is the same as the stock—¾ inch.

Seven slats are evenly spaced along each 23-inch side rail. The total space taken up by the slats is

Fig. 3 *Use these dimensions to mark and cut the slat mortises in the side rails and the underside of the arms. Note that the mortises are the same thickness as the slats but the slats have ¼-inch shoulders.*

seven times 1¼ inches, or 8¾ inches. Subtract that total from 23, and you get 14¼ inches—the length of the rail not taken up by slats. Divide this distance by the number of spaces between slats, making sure to account for the distance between the outer slats and legs: 14¼ inches divided by eight spaces equals 1²⁵⁄₃₂ inches between slats, or roughly 1¾ inches.

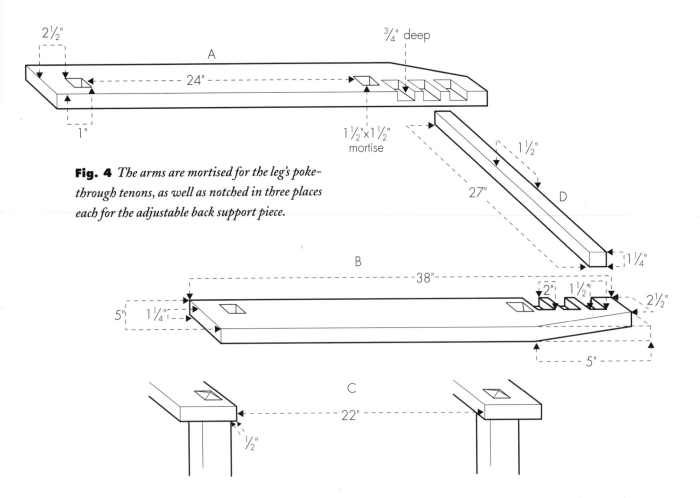

Fig. 4 *The arms are mortised for the leg's poke-through tenons, as well as notched in three places each for the adjustable back support piece.*

Lay out your slats using these calculations, then subtract ¼ inch from either side of these slat lines to get mortise cut lines (see Fig. 3).

Once you have the slat positions measured and marked lightly with a pencil on the two side rails, use a marking gauge to indicate where the ¾-inch mortising bit or router will cut into the rails to make the slat mortises (see pages 34-35). Cutting these mortises will take all your skill (and most of your patience!).

Cutting, Mortising & Notching the Arms

The chair arms are made from 1¼x5-inch oak, cut 38 inches long. The front end of each arm is cut square; the back end of each arm's inside edge is cut square, but the outside edge can be cut square, at an angle (see Fig. 4A and 4B) or, using a jigsaw, cut with a gentle curve that takes off the back outside corner (see the photograph on page 67). If you choose to cut a curve, you can mark it in a number of ways. You can use the gentle curve created by a compass or a flexible piece of thin scrap wood (see page 45), or you can create a complex curve with a "French curve" ruler that has a variety of curve types for guidelines. (If the curve you are cutting is particularly difficult, mark and cut it on one arm, then use that arm as a guide to mark and cut the second arm.)

Each chair arm has two mortises for the legs' poke-through tenons, and either one or seven mortises along its underside for blind tenons for the slats, depending on which style you choose (see Fig. 3).

To determine the position for the mortises that will accommodate the poke-through leg tenons, remember that the side rails have a shoulder-to-shoulder length of 23 inches. The tenon on top of the leg is 1½ inches square, with a ½-inch shoulder. So the 1½-inch-square mortise *center lines* will be 25½ inches apart. They also should be positioned so that the inside of the arm overhangs the inside edge of the leg by ½ inch and overhangs the front edge of the leg by 2 inches (see Fig. 4C). Consequently, the front edge of the mortise will be 2½ inches back from the front edge of the arm (2 inches for the overhang plus ½ inch to account for the shoulder of the leg's tenon). Once you have this front mortise positioned, the inside line to inside line mortise-to-mortise measurement should be 24 inches.

Marking the mortises for the slats is a little trickier. Check these with a slat in position once the arm is mortised for the leg tenons, as you refer to the measurements included in Fig. 3. Once you get a starting point, you can use the same layout pattern illustrated in Fig. 3 on the underside of the arm. Or, to save time, simply rout out a single 18½-inch-long, ¾-inch-wide channel for *all* the slats, instead of cutting mortises for each one. Since this is the underside of the arm, no one will ever see it, and it will save you loads of work.

The Chair Back & Support

While you are working on the arms, cut the notches for the back support piece too. The back of this chair pivots and its angle can be adjusted in three positions for comfort. The "axles" of the back piece are two wooden pins at the base of the chair's back. But the piece that supports the back, about halfway up, is a 1¼x1½x27-inch piece of wood that runs from one arm to the other (see Fig. 4D). It sits in notches that are ¾ inch deep, 1½ inches wide and 2 inches long, so the back support piece will sit higher than the notches. As for their position,

the best approach here is to install the back, pin it to the legs and hold the back support piece in place at various angles to see which are most comfortable. As you determine each of three positions, use a marking gauge to mark the back piece's location on the arms (see Figs. 4A & 4B). It is easiest to cut these notches with a router loaded with a straight bit. Run the router in, say, 1¾ inches, and finish and square up the 2-inch-long notches with a chisel.

The chair back itself is a simple ladder assembly, with two side stiles and three rails (see Fig. 5). The stiles and rails are joined using mortise-and-tenon joints. Since the back assembly has to fit between the chair arms, which are 22 inches apart (see Fig. 4C), make the back assembly 21¾ inches wide so it doesn't scrape against the inside of the arms.

Cut the two stiles for the back assembly from the 2x2-inch oak to a length of 31 inches. (Round the tops with a sander, if you like.) Given that 2x2-inch dimension, the rails' shoulder-to-shoulder distance must be 17¾ inches. The rail stock is ¾x3-inch oak, 17¾ inches long, *plus* the tenon length of 1 inch on each end, making a total of 19¾ inches. The 1-inch-long tenons measure ¾ inch thick and 1½ inches high. There will be a shoulder on two sides only, as the tenons are the same width as the stock.

Position the first rail 3 inches down from the top of the stile. Allow 7 inches between the rails, which will leave ample room for the wooden pins at the base of the stiles (see Fig. 5).

The Pins

The pins can be simple 1-inch-diameter oak dowels, with oak knobs glued on the inside ends to act as stops (see Fig. 5). However, the *real* Mission pins were 1-inch oak dowels with the insertion aspect lathed down to ¾ inch. If you are handy with a lathe, you can make them yourself.

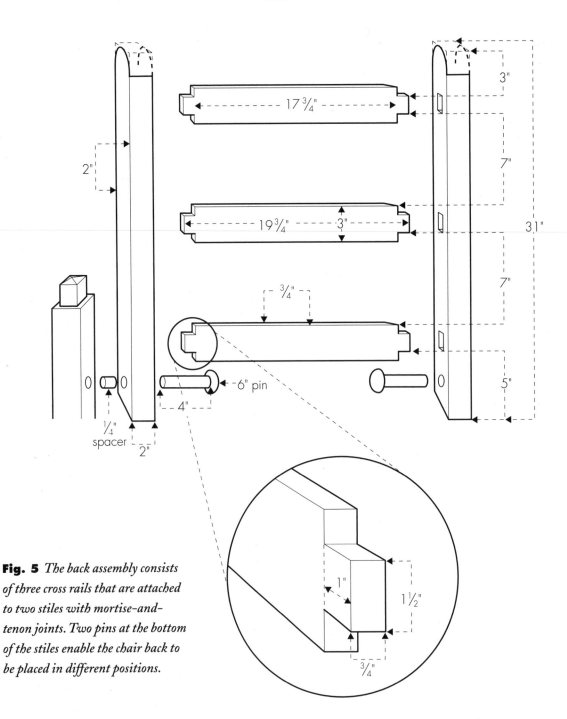

Fig. 5 *The back assembly consists of three cross rails that are attached to two stiles with mortise-and-tenon joints. Two pins at the bottom of the stiles enable the chair back to be placed in different positions.*

Drill a hole, centered, as big as your dowel, through the chair back stiles, 1½ inches up from the bottom (see Fig. 5). Then drill a corresponding hole 2 inches deep into the inside of the legs. Get your dowel and glue ready, but notice that when you install the back of your chair, and "pin" it to the legs, you will see some space between the outside of the chair stiles and the inside of the legs.

This needs to be taken up with a washer or spacer of some kind. Stickley called for a "button" in his original plans, but a ¼-inch-thick brass washer or similarly sized spacing device will do the trick.

Once in place, the pin should not move in the leg hole; fix and glue it into position. But the pin is not glued to the chair back, because the chair back must be able to swivel on it. So position the

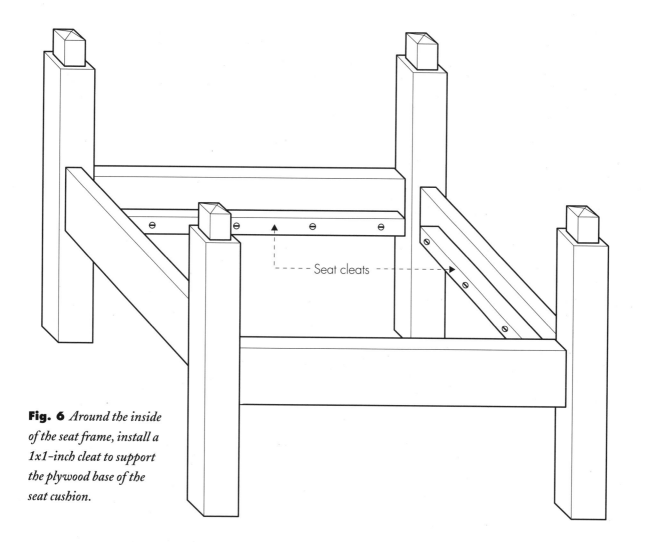

Fig. 6 *Around the inside of the seat frame, install a 1x1-inch cleat to support the plywood base of the seat cushion.*

chair back, insert the pin through it and through the spacer, and *then* glue its end into the hole on the inside face of the leg.

The Cushions

With the chair assembled, it's time to install cleats that will support the plywood base of the seat cushion. Stickley's design called for the seat cushion to be 5 inches thick (and the back cushion to be 6 inches thick). Around the inside faces of the rails, glue and screw four 1x1x23-inch oak strips (see Fig. 6), using 2-inch #8 wood screws per cleat, and predrilling the holes for the screws. When in place, the seat cushion should be an inch or so above the top edge of the front rail, so install the cleats ac-

cordingly. The cushion for the back will not be on a plywood base, but will be a sewn cushion that simply rests on the rails and stiles. To make the seat cushion, see pages 53-55.

Finishing the Morris Chair

Once you have completed the chair, you will have a premiere piece of Mission furniture on your hands, especially worthy of some real care with sanding and finishing. Allow the chair to sit for 24 hours to allow the glue to completely dry, then sand off any blemishes or pencil marks left during the assembly process. Finally, finish this piece as you desire (see pages 47-53).

CHAPTER 13

Couch or "Box Settle"

L ike the dining table and the Morris chair, this couch is a truly definitive piece of Mission furniture, an icon of the era. Despite its intimidating size and heft, this sturdy couch is relatively easy to build and can be used in just about any room (if it fits!). It is designed for an upholstered seat cushion only, so use throw pillows for the back (see photograph, page 69). Before starting this project, check your work site carefully and make sure that the couch will fit out the door after it is assembled *and* in the door where it will be used. The couch will be about 3 feet wide.

The real challenge here is handling the long, heavy pieces of lumber when cutting mortises and tenons. Because of their sizes, they are particularly unwieldy, and you may find you need out-feed support tables for your equipment to hold up the far end of longer lumber stock.

The best way to approach a project of this size is by looking at it section by section, and then breaking down those sections into their component pieces.

CUT LIST AND MATERIALS

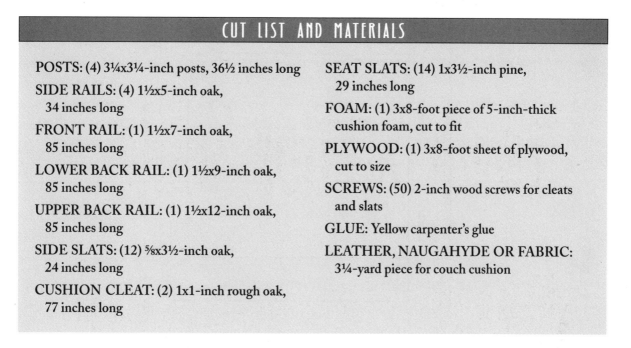

POSTS: (4) 3¼x3¼-inch posts, 36½ inches long

SIDE RAILS: (4) 1½x5-inch oak, 34 inches long

FRONT RAIL: (1) 1½x7-inch oak, 85 inches long

LOWER BACK RAIL: (1) 1½x9-inch oak, 85 inches long

UPPER BACK RAIL: (1) 1½x12-inch oak, 85 inches long

SIDE SLATS: (12) ⅝x3½-inch oak, 24 inches long

CUSHION CLEAT: (2) 1x1-inch rough oak, 77 inches long

SEAT SLATS: (14) 1x3½-inch pine, 29 inches long

FOAM: (1) 3x8-foot piece of 5-inch-thick cushion foam, cut to fit

PLYWOOD: (1) 3x8-foot sheet of plywood, cut to size

SCREWS: (50) 2-inch wood screws for cleats and slats

GLUE: Yellow carpenter's glue

LEATHER, NAUGAHYDE OR FABRIC: 3¼-yard piece for couch cushion

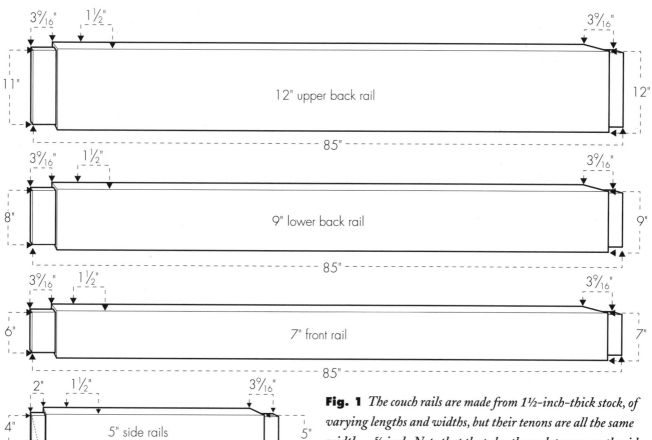

Fig. 1 *The couch rails are made from 1½-inch-thick stock, of varying lengths and widths, but their tenons are all the same width— ⅝ inch. Note that the poke-through tenons on the side rails are 3/16 inches long and the blind tenons are 2 inches long, except for the upper back end tenons, which are trimmed at an angle to accommodate the upper back rail position.*

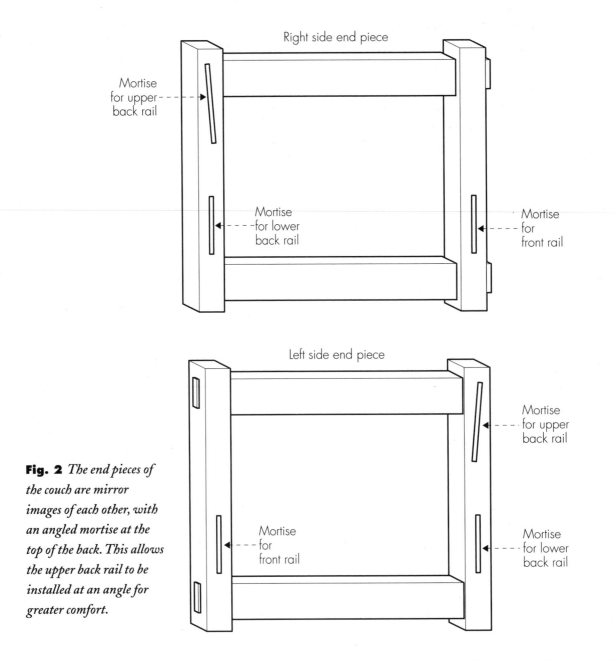

Fig. 2 *The end pieces of the couch are mirror images of each other, with an angled mortise at the top of the back. This allows the upper back rail to be installed at an angle for greater comfort.*

The Rails,
Side Pieces & Posts

The couch has three kinds of rails (see Fig. 1): a single front rail, upper and lower back rails, and four side rails—two at each end. All are cut with tenons that will be inserted into mortises in the four posts.

The four side rails attach to the posts to create end pieces (see Fig. 2). If you look closely, you'll see that the end pieces are mirror images of each other. When they are in position, the mortise for the upper back rail is angled so the rail slopes back at a slight angle. This makes the couch much more comfortable. (These cuts are rather tricky and must be accurate; refer frequently to the drawings to help visualize how the end pieces are positioned so the upper back rail is tilted in the proper direction.)

The original period Mission plans call for four 36½-inch-long posts that measure 3¼ inches square, but it will be hard to find a single piece of oak with those exact dimensions (unless you custom-order it). And to mill down a larger piece would be difficult as well (and the stock would be *frighteningly* expensive). So the best thing to do is to assemble and "glue up" each post using four ⅞x3¼-inch pieces of oak stock (see pages 44-45). After the post has dried, it may have an actual dimension very close to 3¼ inches square, but if it doesn't, you can mill it down by running it lengthwise through your table saw.

Tip: When dealing with four identical pieces of wood that will be used for uprights, yet don't have identical cuts, it's important to keep track of which one goes where. So before you do any cutting into the posts, the first step is to mark where the posts will sit in the final furniture assembly. Gather all four posts together so they make a square. Then, draw a small square on the end grains in the center of the square, where the posts are adjacent, and number each post. Later, if you get confused as to which one goes where, you can easily reposition the post in its proper alignment by simply looking at the square and checking the post's number (see Fig. 3).

The Tenons

Though the tenons are cut out of different-sized lumber, making the tenons different widths, all of the poke-through tenons will protrude the same distance through the posts, so the poke-through tenon *length* will not change from rail to rail. All of the poke-through tenons in this couch design are 3⁹⁄₁₆ inches long. This dimension is computed by adding the post width (3¼ inches) plus the poke-through distance (⁵⁄₁₆ inch). If you are using a post that is more than 3¼ inches thick, be sure to account for your increased width by lengthening the tenon; otherwise, it won't poke through, and it

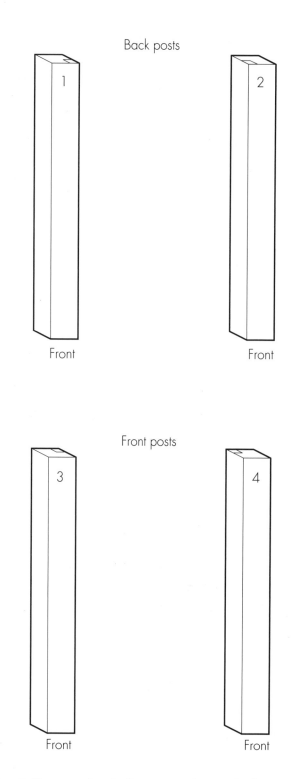

Fig. 3 *To ensure that the four posts, or legs, are in the correct position when cutting the various mortises, first gather them together to make a square, draw a small box in the center where they meet and then label them 1, 2, 3 or 4.*

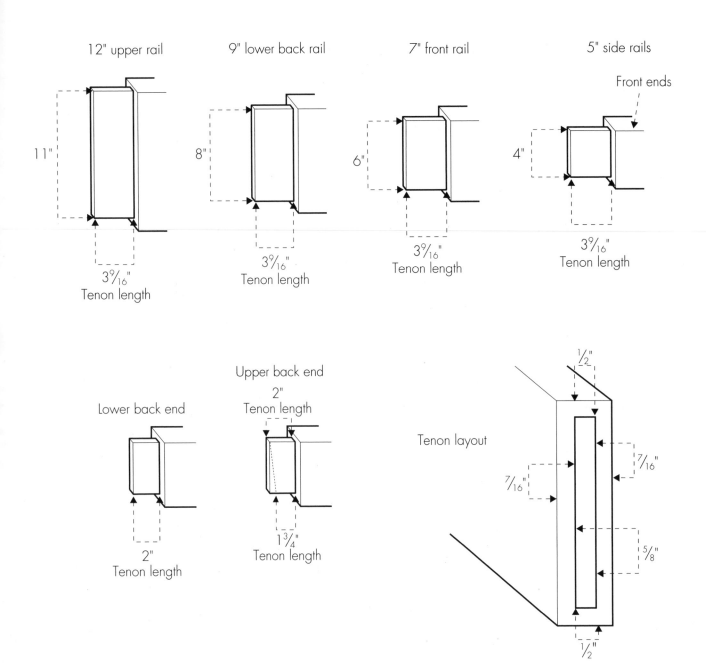

Fig. 4 *The tenons for each of the rails have different heights, but they all have ½-inch shoulders and are ⅝ inch thick.*

might even end up recessed, which would look terrible. Each poke-through tenon also has a ½-inch shoulder and is ⅝ inch thick (see Fig. 4).

The four blind tenons where the side rails meet the back side posts are cut to these same dimensions (½-inch shoulders, ⅝ inch thick), but are only 2 inches long instead of 3⁹⁄₁₆ inches. However, if you make the tenons for the back ends of the upper rails 2 inches long, they will block the insertion of the ends of the long upper back rail coming in perpen-

dicular to them. Trim the bottom end of these two blind tenons to fit them into this joint. Angle the tenon here to fit, making it 1¾ inches at one end, angled up to its full 2-inch length on the other (see Fig. 4). Using a router or table saw (see pages 36-37), cut the tenons for all the rails.

The Mortises

All of the mortise cuts are bored in either the posts (for the rails running the length of the couch and for the side rails) or in the side rails (for the six slats that are on each side of the couch). Not all the mortises are for poke-through tenons, though; some are for blind tenons, as mentioned previously. You'll find blind tenons for *rails* in the four locations already noted: two where the top side rails join the back posts and two where the bottom side rails join the back posts. Blind tenons for *slats* are found where they join with the side rails at the top and bottom. All other mortises go all the way through the posts. Figs. 5 and 6 show the mortise cuts that are needed to accommodate the poke-through and blind tenons on the posts. The mortises for the upper two back ends of the side rails intersect the mortise for the back top rail. This intersection dictates the length of the tenon, as explained above.

Since there are four different-sized rails, there need to be four different-sized mortises to fit the rail tenons, as mortise sizes are dictated by the tenon sizes. However, every tenon (and thus the resulting mortise), no matter what size the rail, is ⅝ inch thick in this couch design. Referring to Figs. 5 and 6, lay out all the mortises, and cut them with a router or mortising bit on a drill press (see pages 34-36).

If you use a router, you will have to rout on one side of the post, then flip the post over and rout on the opposite side to fashion the mortises for the poke-through tenons. These routed mortises should meet exactly in the middle, in much the same way that two tunnel diggers working toward each other from opposite directions should meet exactly in the middle. To make the mortises for the blind tenons, however, you will rout out only one side of the wood. Once the routing is completed, clean out the mortise with a chisel and blow out any sawdust left behind.

The Side Rails & Slats

The last pieces to cut are the slats and the side rail mortises. Using a table saw, cut 12 slats from the ⅝x3½-inch oak, each measuring 24 inches in length (see Fig. 7).

Next, rout the rails to receive the slats. There are two things to remember here. First, make sure you rout the *underside* of the top rail and the *top side* of the bottom rail, and second, note that the mortises are the same size as the slats; these slats don't have shoulders.

Using a marking gauge (see pages 34-35) and referring to the dimensions shown in Fig. 7, lay out the slat mortises for the rails. Set the router depth to ¾ inch, plus at least ¹⁄₁₆ inch deeper, or about ⅞ inch total. Note that the ⅝x3½-inch slots are centered on the rail, with ⅞ inch between each slot; the outermost slots are ¾ inch in from the edge of the body of the rail.

Assembling the Couch

With all the pieces cut and mortises completed, get your glue, bar or pipe clamps (see page 26) and a rubber mallet. Start by gluing up and assembling the slats and side rails. Use a square to make sure the assembly isn't racked, measuring its length end-for-end to double-check that it is square. You want the distance from the upper rail to the lower rail on the left side of the assembly to exactly match the distance between the upper rail to the lower rail on the right side of the assembly. Also, check to make sure the same length is exposed on each slat: about 22½ inches. Draw the assembly together with the bar or pipe clamps, and be sure to clean off any excess glue before it has a chance to dry. Let the side pieces dry the amount of time recommended by the glue manufacturer, or at least one hour, before moving on to the next step.

After you have the slats and rails assembled and

(continued on page 132)

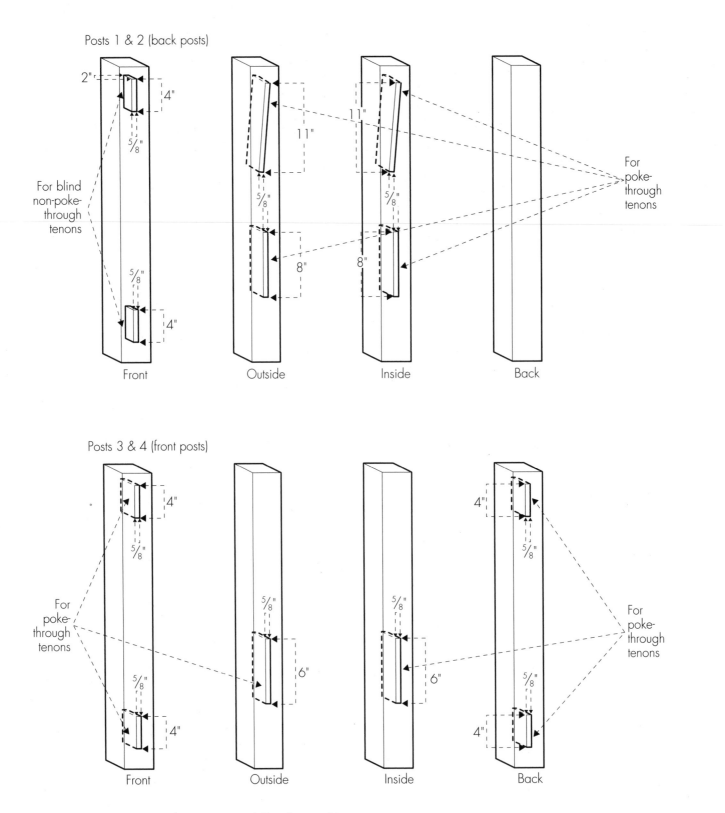

Fig. 5 *Study these drawings carefully when marking the mortise cuts on the legs. Note that 1 and 2 refer to the back posts and 3 and 4 to the front.*

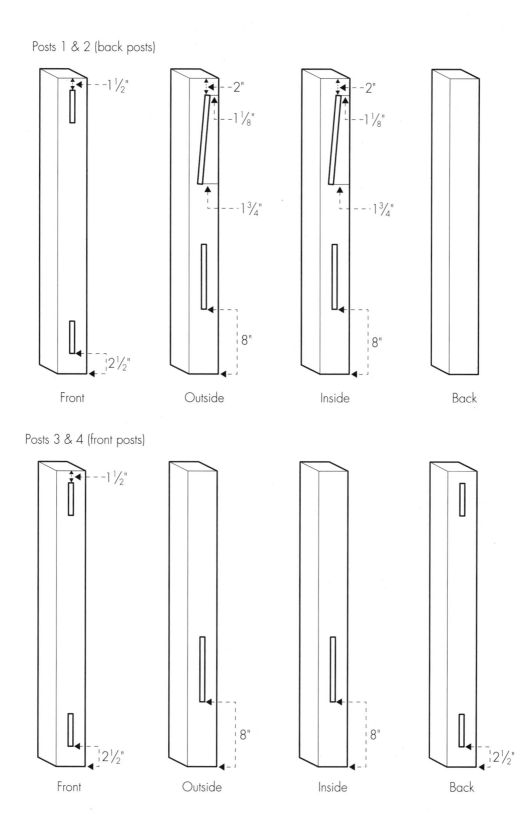

Posts 1 & 2 (back posts)

Front   Outside   Inside   Back

Posts 3 & 4 (front posts)

Front   Outside   Inside   Back

Fig. 6 *When positioning the mortises, use these dimensions to determine their distances from the ends of the posts.*

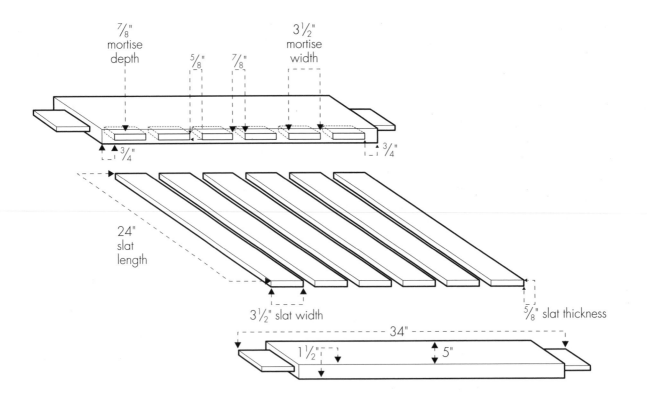

Fig. 7 *Cut mortises into the side rails using the dimensions shown here. The mortises are the same size as the slats, with no shoulders. Each slat is ⅝ inch thick and ⅞ inch apart from each other, with a ¾-inch space on the ends.*

the glue has set up, attach these side pieces to the posts, being careful to work both rail tenons into the mortises evenly; otherwise, you'll rack the slat-and-rail assembly. Now you have both end pieces assembled. Let the assembly sit for another hour to allow the glue to dry.

The next step is a two-person job, because the front, lower back and upper back rails have to be inserted at the same time. Glue the rails' tenons, and insert all three rails into one end piece. (This can be done most easily by laying the end piece flat on the floor and dropping the rails into place.) Then glue the rails' tenons on the opposite end, stand the other end piece upright into place and insert the rails. Slowly and carefully rap the end pieces with a rubber mallet until the tenons pro-

trude ⁵⁄₁₆ inch. When all the tenons protrude the same length, that is an indication that your couch is square. You can double-check for square by measuring across the front and back of the couch. The distance between the tops of the posts should equal the distance between the bottoms of the posts. (Another way to check for square is by taking diagonal measurements from front left to back right and front right to back left. These lengths should be identical.) If not, go back and whack the post(s) with a mallet *before the glue dries.* When you are finished, let the glue dry thoroughly before moving on to the next step. This is particularly important, since you are not clamping the assembly together at this point in the process.

Preparing the Seat

The upholstered seat cushion sits on slats that rest on cleats. The cleats are screwed into the inside faces of the front and lower back rails. To position the cleats, first determine how thick a cushion you

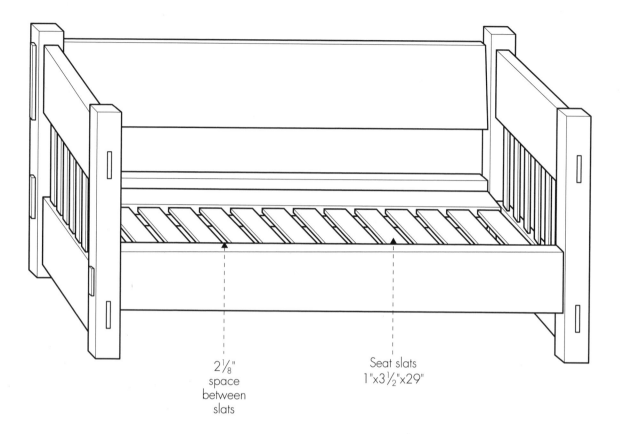

2⅛"
space
between
slats

Seat slats
1"x3½"x29"

14 slats, with end slats flush to outside

Fig. 8 *When the couch is assembled, install a cleat on the front and lower back rails, and screw 14 pine slats to the cleats to support the seat cushion.*

are going to use for your seat. You want to ensure that the front rail doesn't push up into the underside of your knees when you sit on the cushion and compress it with your weight. So, if you are using a 5-inch-thick foam cushion, you want the cleats positioned 3 or 4 inches below the top of the front rail. When the slats are in place, the cushion will actually be raised up an inch or so above the front rail. When you have the front cleat positioned, run a level to the lower back rail and mark the location for the cleats there.

For the cleat stock, predrill and screw in place a 1x1-inch oak strip 77 inches long. Use 2-inch wood screws every 8 inches or so. Screw the cleat to the inside faces of the lower back and front rails

only, not the side rails. (Be especially careful to use the correct length screws so they don't go all the way through the front or back rails.) For the seat slats, cut fourteen 1x3½-inch pieces of pine, 29 inches long. Put the first slats at either end of the couch, flush to the outside of the cleats, and space the remaining ones 2⅛ inches from one another (see Fig. 8). Screw the slats into the cleats with 2-inch wood screws. (If the pine starts to split, predrill the holes.)

Finishing the Couch

With the couch assembly complete, now is the time to clean it up with a final sanding. Sand off any pencil marks or blemishes the piece picked up during assembly. Then turn to pages 47-55 for instructions on how to stain or fume the couch and make the seat cushion.

RESOURCES

Books

Furniture of the American Arts and Crafts Movement: Stickley and Roycroft Mission Oak, by David M. Cathers. New American Library, New York, NY. 1984.

Joining Wood, by Nick Engler. Rodale Press, Emmaus, PA. 1992.

Arts and Crafts, by James Massey and Shirley Maxwell. Abbeville Press, New York, NY. 1995.

Routing and Shaping, by Nick Engler. Rodale Press, Emmaus, PA. 1992.

The Arts and Crafts Movement: A Study of Its Sources, Ideals, and Influence on Design Theory, by Naylor Gillian. MIT Press, Cambridge, MA. 1971.

The Collected Works of Gustav Stickley, Stephen Gray and Robert Edwards, eds. (catalog reprint). Turn of the Century Editions, New York, NY. 1981.

Official Price Guide to Arts and Crafts, by Bruce Johnson. House of Collectibles, New York, NY. 1992.

The Pegged Joint, by Bruce Johnson. Knock on Wood, Asheville, NC. 1995.

The Arts and Crafts Movement in America 1876-1916, by Judson R. Clark. Princeton University Press, Princeton, NJ. 1972.

In the Arts and Crafts Style, by Barbara Mayer. Chronicle Books, San Francisco, CA. 1993.

Mission Furniture: How to Make It, by Popular Mechanics Company. Dover Publications, New York, NY. 1980.

The Furniture of Gustav Stickley, by Thomas Mossman and Joseph Bavaro. Linden Publishing, Fresno, CA. 1982.

The Craftsman: An Anthology, Barry Sanders, ed. Peregrine Smith Inc., Salt Lake City, UT. 1978.

Gustav Stickley, The Craftsman, by Mary Ann Smith. Dover Publications, New York, NY. 1983.

Making Authentic Craftsman Furniture, by Gustav Stickley (selected reprints from *The Craftsman*). Dover Publications, New York, NY. 1986.

Treasures of the American Arts and Crafts Movement 1890-1920, by Tod M. Volpe and Beth Cathers. Harry N. Abrams, New York, NY. 1988.

Periodicals

American Bungalow
P.O. Box 756
Sierra Madre, CA 91025-0756

The Craftsman Homeowner Club Newsletter
31 South Grove Street
East Aurora, NY 14052
716-652-3333

Fine Woodworking
Taunton Press
P.O. Box 5506
Newtown, CT 06470-5506
800-926-8776

Style 1900
17 South Main Street
Lambertville, NJ 08530
609-397-4104

Places to Visit

Roycroft Campus, Inn and Shops
40 South Grove Street
East Aurora, NY 14052
716-652-5552

Craftsman Farms
2352 Route 10, West
Parsippany, NJ 07054
201-540-1165

Grove Park Inn
290 Macon Avenue
Asheville, NC 28804
800-438-5800

Gamble House
4 Westmoreland Place
Pasadena, CA 91103
818-793-3334

ABOUT THE AUTHOR

John D. Wagner is an award-winning author of five other books, including *Building Adirondack Furniture, Building a Multi-Use Barn, House Framing* and *The Complete Guide to Drywall.* As a free-lance journalist, he has authored hundreds of articles on furniture making, architectural history, and construction and wood-working techniques. He is past features editor for *The Journal of Light Construction* and currently is a contributing editor for *Tools of the Trade* and *The Journal of Light Construction.* Also a published poet and travel essayist, John lives with his wife, Leita M. Hancock, in Montpelier, Vermont.